W9-CPC-057

# ((( overheard )))
## in the office

# ((overheard))
## in the office

Conversations from Water Coolers,
Conference Rooms, and Cubicles

**S. Morgan Friedman and Michael Malice**

A Perigee Book

**A PERIGEE BOOK**
**Published by the Penguin Group**
**Penguin Group (USA) Inc.**
**375 Hudson Street, New York, New York 10014, USA**

Penguin Group (Canada), 90 Eglinton Avenue East, Suite 700, Toronto, Ontario M4P 2Y3, Canada (a division of Pearson Penguin Canada Inc.) • Penguin Books Ltd., 80 Strand, London WC2R 0RL, England • Penguin Group Ireland, 25 St. Stephen's Green, Dublin 2, Ireland (a division of Penguin Books Ltd.) • Penguin Group (Australia), 250 Camberwell Road, Camberwell, Victoria 3124, Australia (a division of Pearson Australia Group Pty. Ltd.) • Penguin Books India Pvt. Ltd., 11 Community Centre, Panchsheel Park, New Delhi—110 017, India • Penguin Group (NZ), 67 Apollo Drive, Rosedale, North Shore 0632, New Zealand (a division of Pearson New Zealand Ltd.) • Penguin Books (South Africa) (Pty.) Ltd., 24 Sturdee Avenue, Rosebank, Johannesburg 2196, South Africa

Penguin Books Ltd., Registered Offices: 80 Strand, London WC2R 0RL, England

While the author has made every effort to provide accurate telephone numbers and Internet addresses at the time of publication, neither the publisher nor the author assumes any responsibility for errors, or for changes that occur after publication. Further, the publisher does not have any control over and does not assume any responsibility for author or third-party websites or their content.

Copyright © 2008 by S. Morgan Friedman and Michael Malice
Cover art and design by Ben Gibson
Text design by Tiffany Estreicher

All rights reserved.
No part of this book may be reproduced, scanned, or distributed in any printed or electronic form without permission. Please do not participate in or encourage piracy of copyrighted materials in violation of the author's rights. Purchase only authorized editions.
PERIGEE is a registered trademark of Penguin Group (USA) Inc.
The "P" design is a trademark belonging to Penguin Group (USA) Inc.

First edition: February 2008

Library of Congress Cataloging-in-Publication Data

Overheard in the office : conversations from water coolers, conference rooms, and cubicles / [compiled by] S. Morgan Friedman and Michael Malice.
    p.   cm.
  ISBN-13: 978-0-399-53391-4
  1. Work—Humor.   2. Offices—Humor.   I. Friedman, S. Morgan.   II. Malice, Michael.
  PN6231.W644094 2008
  818'.602—dc22                                                    2007038062

PRINTED IN THE UNITED STATES OF AMERICA

10   9   8   7   6   5   4   3   2   1

Most Perigee books are available at special quantity discounts for bulk purchases for sales promotions, premiums, fund-raising, or educational use. Special books, or book excerpts, can also be created to fit specific needs. For details, write: Special Markets, Penguin Group (USA) Inc., 375 Hudson Street, New York, New York 10014.

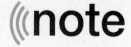**note**

This book reproduces statements and comments overheard in offices around the world. They are presented as heard, without any attempt to edit or censor, the objective being to give the reader an unscientific but revealing peek at the private opinions held by office workers. Some readers may find certain statements hurtful, outrageous, or offensive. In publishing this material, however, neither the authors nor the publisher intends in any way to endorse or advance any of the viewpoints expressed. This book is simply a slice of real life, for better or for worse.

# ((thanks

This book would not have been possible without eaves-droppers in offices around the world, as well as everyone else who has made this book possible, including Michael Bourret, Alvaro Casanova, Adina Cepler, Dan Horwitz, Meg Leder, Arthur Lehman, Joaquin Perez, Julian Porta, Jenny Weiss, and Uncle Walter. A special thanks to Dave Barnette, Adam Holland, Danielle Lindemann, and Nick Saint, who wrote the headlines for most of the quotes in this book, and Kristina Ryan, who edited all of them.

# ((contents

# (((introduction

There's something different about eavesdropping in the office.

When you're eavesdropping on the street, you are anonymous. The eavesdropee is anonymous. You two will probably never meet again. You may make eye contact, but *so what*? It doesn't matter. You can just smile and walk away.

But the office is a different story, a self-contained environment. You'll probably see the people sitting around you five days every week for the next few years, maybe even for the rest of your life. These include your boss, who is—of course—far stupider than you, and your coworkers, who are just downright incompetent, but who you somehow have to manage to deal with every day in order to get anything done.

The office, in other words, is its own little universe, with its own actors, dramas, and stage. Unlike eavesdropping on the street, in the office you can't ignore, forget, or mercilessly mock those around you—at least, not to their faces.

Into this world, Overheard in the Office was born. The website began as a mere outlet, where you could let out your frustration over everyone, from the VP of technology, who doesn't know how to use a computer, on down. And up. A place where you could share in the frustration of your fellow cubicle-bound workers around the world, reminded every moment that your boss isn't the only stupid one out there. *They're all like that.*

But as the website grew, and our favorite quotes evolved into a book, *something changed.* The site that began as a mere chronicle of idiocy matured into, well, a chronicle of our lives. We spend more time in the office than we do with our friends, with our extended families, with the girls and guys we date casually. The office is our world. *Overheard in the Office* is an outlet to help us deal with this world.

And it's a great outlet. It reminds us that our own coworkers and bosses aren't the only insane ones out there. It's not a fictional parody of the office, the way our favorite TV shows and movies are. It actually *is The Office*, whether it's in California, Ohio, Canada, Singapore, Australia, or anywhere else in the world.

And, most important, it makes us laugh at everything and everyone.

—*The Editors, Team Overhead*

P.S. One significant change has been made between the site and the book: We have agreed to use the idiosyncratic spelling of "Canada" to refer to our northern neighbor— rather than the more standard "Canadia"—in order to avoid a reenactment of that Library of Alexandria fiasco.

((( **bosses**

## Use the Shank Key

Vice president using Instant Messenger: How do I type a smiley face that means "I'll cut you"?

*550 Madison Avenue, New York, New York*

## Actually, He's Leaving Reminders for Himself on His Voicemail

Office manager on phone: Which one of Mommy's boyfriends beat you badly enough as a child to turn you into the bitter, empty, hollow shell of a human being you are today?

Supervisor to trainee: See? That's why we have to answer the phone quickly in this office—to keep the managers from picking up the phone. Ever.

*221 Corporate Gateway Boulevard, Columbia, South Carolina*

## Nobody Who Says "Languish" Would Ever Get Promoted in the U.S.

Boss: So, I have a problem with giving you the job even though I know you can do it.

Worker: What's the issue?

Boss: You seem to be annoyed with us, and you're not upbeat enough after what happened.

Worker: What happened is that I lived the values, delivered on everything, then the organization totally screwed me over, gave my job to someone else, and left me to languish for a year with no certainty about my future. Now you're saying you can't give me another job because you've been such dickheads?

Boss: I know it sounds bad . . .

*388 George Street, Sydney, Australia*

## No, I Still Work Here

Boss: Do you know what the difference between you and me is?

Employee: About twenty IQ points and a sense of style?

*1 Lincoln Plaza, New York, New York*

## How Does Me Killing You and Assuming Your Identity Sound?

Boss: I found this [correspondence dated a week ago] in my inbox waiting for my signature. It was Bill Smith's* estate tax return! Why didn't you tell me to *check my inbox*?! There's all kinds of stuff in there that hasn't gone out. You have to come up with a way for me to check my inbox more regularly so things like this don't happen again!

Secretary: Um, okay . . . Do you want me to set Outlook reminders that you'll ignore, or would you like to ignore me personally?

*900 East Hill Avenue, Knoxville, Tennessee*

*Asterisks throughout the book indicate that real names have been changed.

## He's Still Using a Sundial

Boss: Call England and find out what time it is.

Assistant: Call who in England? England is five hours ahead of us, so it's 4:17 there.

Boss: Can you please *listen* to what I have to say and just *call* England? I need to be sure.

Assistant, two minutes later: I called England, and it's 4:19.

Boss: See, it pays to double-check. You were two minutes off.

*1345 Avenue of the Americas, New York, New York*

## And Then I'll Blow Up His Car

Boss to employee: Well, I'm outta here! Too bad you have to stay!

Janitor: You're not letting him leave early?

Boss: No. I'm the boss—I get to go. He has to stay.

Janitor: Okay. Well, bye.

Boss: Bye! [He leaves.]

Janitor to employee: So, you're leaving in five minutes, right?

Employee: I'll wait till he clears the building.

*59 Maiden Lane, New York, New York*

## It Just Has to Make Money; It Doesn't Have to Make Sense

Woman: Isn't this the most fucking idiotic thing you've ever had to do in your life?

Senior vice president: No, actually, which is really embarrassing.

*120 West 106th Street, New York, New York*

## Because God Know Mine Am Bad

Manager: We're hiring another producer in Quebec. And one thing that I think we all agree on is that his English has to be very, very well.

*180 Varick Street, New York, New York*

## Or Close Enough. It's Not Really Super Important.

Vice president: Well, we'll just keep compromising until we reach mediocrity.

*139 Townsend Street, San Francisco, California*

## What Really Happened to IBM

Project manager: Because of their dependencies, these two projects should be run in parallel.
CEO: Yeah, we need to paralyze them. Good idea, Ted*!

*Chicago, Illinois*

## My Soul Has Filed for Chapter 11

Manager #1: So, how'd that meeting go? Are you still morally bankrupt?
Manager #2: Why, yes! Yes, I am!

*750 Broadway, New York, New York*

## All That Remains Since We Can No Longer Surf for Porn on the Job

Employee: Hey, I know it's the end of the day on Friday, but I'm really bored. Do you have anything for me to do?
Boss: Oh! Here, have some bubble wrap!

*137 4th Avenue, Edmonton, Alabama*


## And Susan Was Maimed. Isn't That Great?

Boss: I wouldn't even be able to kill myself right today. I'd screw it up.
Employee: If it makes you feel better, I knocked myself unconscious this weekend.
Boss: Yeah, actually, it does.

*323 East Grand River Avenue, Howell, Michigan*


## I Quit, Asshole! . . . I Think It's a Jelly Glazed, but I Can't Tell for Sure.

Division chief: Why are you wearing a visitor pass? What happened to your badge?
Editor: Hey, fuck you! I brought in doughnuts!
Division chief: How dare you talk to me like that?! . . . Is that a Boston cream?

*Pentagon, 48 North Rotary Road, Arlington, Virginia*

## And Welcome to the Federal Civil Service

Recent business school grad: You know, working for this company is not for the weak of heart. There is not a lot of recognition handed out to people.

Senior executive: Recognition? You want recognition? You are a dumbass. How's that?

*Niagara-on-the-Lake, Ontario, Canada*


## Who Wants to Work in a Dump Like This Anyway?

Manager: We're going to have to let you go.

Employee: I didn't do nothin'!

Manager: I personally caught you defecating into the employee bathroom sink.

Employee: The toilet was filthy!

*95 South Illinois Street, Indianapolis, Indiana*


## He Runs a Brothel

Supervisor: Different day, same shit.

Employee: That's my favorite saying! "Different day, same shit."

Supervisor: We probably shouldn't swear. . . . I don't want to offend the customers.

Employee: Probably.

Supervisor: You know what my favorite saying is? "Fuck that!"

*Mount Prospect, Illinois*

## Which Is the Legal Definition of "Best Lawyer"

Boss: We need a lawyer to handle this. If it were five years ago I'd call my brother. He was one of the best lawyers in the country, but he can't help me anymore because he's been disbarred.

*Midtown, New York, New York*

## Where Do You Think I'm Calling You From?

Boss on speakerphone: So, I need you to give me those files, like, in five minutes.

Employee: Um . . .

Boss on speakerphone: I'm serious. I want them in my hand in five minutes.

Employee: You know that I work at home, right?

Boss on speakerphone: So?

Employee: So, I live forty-five minutes away from your so-called office . . . Speaking of which, did you ever get that toilet out of the hallway?

*3207 Hayloft Court, Frederick, Maryland*

## The First-Ever Suggestion That College Leads to Sobriety

Woman: Man, I got so shit-faced last night. Major hangover. I'm not gonna get anything done.

Lackey: Well, good thing you're a VP. You can get away with that kind of thing.

Woman: I know, right? And I don't even have a college education!

Lackey: Guess I wasted those four years and workday so-briety for nothing. And all this time I could have been a hungover dropout.

Woman: Live and learn!

*Providence, Rhode Island*


## That's Different from What He Said Last Week at the Office Party

Boss: Does anyone have any questions? [Employee asks involved question.] You know what? I have a million questions that you cannot answer.

Employee: But you asked if anyone had any questions.

Boss: Yeah, and if I asked if anyone had to go to the bath-room, I wouldn't expect you to whip it out and take a whiz right here.

*Stamford, Connecticut*


## First, Break the Employee's Legs, Then Criticize the Way He Walks

General manager: How were your days off?

Supervisor: Pretty good. Did some hiking.

General manager: How was the conference?

Supervisor: What conference?

General manager: I emailed you Wednesday about the loss prevention meeting on Thursday morning. I know it was short notice.

Supervisor: Thursday was my day off. Wednesday was my day off. I wasn't here to check my emails.

General manager: So you didn't go to the mandatory meeting?

Supervisor: Um . . .

General manager: You have to check your email every day. No excuses.

Supervisor: I wasn't here to check my email.

General manager: No excuses.

*687 12th Street, Gresham, Oregon*


## Receptionists Have a Limited Ability to Extrapolate

Manager: It is important that you put any call through to me today—my mother-in-law is dying.

Receptionist: Is she okay?

Manager: No, she's dying.

*Davey Street, Hobart, Australia*


## It All Started Back in My Mother's Fallopian Tube . . .

Boss: Why do you look so sad?

Employee: You really want to know?

Boss: No.

*Toledo, Ohio*


## For Murphy, It's Skywriters or Nothing

Suit: It's been a big thing. I've sent a bunch of emails about it.

Boss: Yeah, I've ignored them. Sorry.

*Los Angeles, California*

## I Thought You'd Never Ask!

Salesman: . . . And then you're cruising for a bruising.
Sales manager: How old are you?
Salesman: What?
Sales manager: Cruising for a bruising? My grandma said that!
Salesman: How about, "Truckin' for a fuckin' "?
Sales manager: Okay.

*111 Oak Street, Bonner Springs, Kansas*

## Well, It Is and It Isn't

Supervisor: She used to wear all sorts of things in her hair, and then one day she showed up with a condom and we were like, "Honey, that's not a Scrunchie."

*473 Ridge Road, Dayton, New Jersey*

## Exactly What We Need to Jump-Start Our Marketing Campaign

Marketing director: There's one student there I'd love to get a photo of. She's drop-dead gorgeous and hardly ever wears clothes.

*16340 North Scottsdale Road, Scottsdale, Arizona*

bosses

## Hey, That Loaf of Rye Was Totally Coming on to Me!

Boss: That's what I hate about these people who take the Bible literally—it's so pick-and-choose! What about all the parts where you get stoned for looking at bread the wrong way?

*Print shop, Sunset Park, Brooklyn, New York*


## And I Have Seen Enough

Office grunt: Wow! Look at the legs on that chick! Those are some really short shorts! Look, Bill*!
Boss: Yeah, that's my wife.

*740 4th Street, Santa Rosa, California*


## Actually, It's a Generational Rorschach Test

Twenty-ish newbie: Why is there a Harry Potter picture in our lobby?
Forty-ish manager: Actually, that's a painting of John Lennon.

*Silicon Valley, California*


## They're Just Mad about the Whole "Canadia" Thing

CEO: I read a study that said that 50 percent of Canadians disapprove of Americans.

Employee: Yeah, I guess they just don't agree with many of the U.S.'s recent actions.

CEO: No, it's because they're jealous of Americans.

Employee: Errr, that's perhaps a somewhat U.S.-centric view . . .

CEO: I've been to Canada. I've seen it firsthand. They are very jealous of us.

Employee: Actually, now that you mention it, I'm surprised it was only 50 percent.

*Frederick, Maryland*

## "Fuck You" Was More of a Request Than an Expletive

Manager: Can you gather up the other guys? We have to move a bunch of stuff.

Employee: Fuck you.

Manager: What did you just say to me?

Employee: Fuck you, asshole.

Manager: Are you nuts?

Employee: Fuck you, bitch.

Manager: You're fired. Get out of here.

Employee: I wasn't clocked in. You can't fire me.

Manager walks to computer, clocks him in: You're fired. [Clocks him out.]

Employee: That's so unfair.

*Circle Centre Mall, Indianapolis, Indiana*

## From the Runaway Bestseller *Affirmations for Stupid People*

Manager to himself: I am a ball of fire. I am a *ball of fire!*

*Eugene, Oregon*

## If You Unfocus Your Eyes Just Right, You Can See One of Those "Magic" Pictures

Worker: Cliff's* balls are hanging out of his shorts.

Manager: Yeah, he's got real hangers.

Worker: You should tell him.

Manager: I like it. No one else can see it, and it's his lunch break. Besides, you've been looking at his scrotum for the last ten minutes.

*Balboa Park, San Diego, California*

## It's Where the Porn Stars Go

Manager: Yeah, so at this new salon I can get my hair highlighted for a hundred and twenty bucks, and that includes the shampoo, haircut, and blow job.

*Bethesda, Maryland*

## After Delegating His Memory to Abby, Frank Experienced Difficulty with Remote Access

Boss on phone: Abby,* it's Frank.* I'm at the British Library, and there's a man looking at me.

Abby: Yes?

Boss: Who is it?

*British Library, 96 Euston Road, London, England*

## Stephen's Retroactive Skill with Metaphors Did Not Go Unnoticed in His Quarterly Review

Vice president: Yeah, and if we go over there we could get all our stuff back. We have a whole bunch of equipment in China stuck in escargot.

Director: Um . . . You mean *escrow*?

Vice president: What did I say? Escargot? Well, that works, too, since it's so slow in getting back to us.

Director: Sure it does.

*45th Street & 9th Avenue, New York, New York*

## How Angie Got Her First Job

Manager: So, why do you want to work in a bookstore?

Teen: Um . . . I love reading books.

Manager: What's the last book you read?

Teen: Uh . . . Ummm . . . I don't . . . [Giggles.] . . . Ummm . . .

Manager: Well, what's your favorite book?

Teen: Um . . .

Manager: Okay.

*Barnes & Noble, Irving Mall, Irving, Texas*

bosses

## Well, You Guys Are the Engineers, So If You Say It Needs to Be Made Out of Platinum . . .

Tech: So, do you think that we should go for this project?

Boss: Absolutely. The client is ridiculously stupid, but they are open-minded.

*London, England*

## Of Course, If We Fire Her We'll Have the Expense of Training Another Screamer

General manager: Should we fire Missy*? She was scream-ing at you in front of other employees.

Manager #1: I don't know. What does Missy feel we should do to her?

General manager: Uh, I didn't ask her.

Manager #2: She thinks we should buy her a pizza and give her a raise. What the fuck do you think she feels we should do to her?

*Indianapolis, Indiana*

## Ummm . . . It Shows Respect to the President

Manager: My new BM is awesome!

Subordinate: You mean BMW . . . The *W* is important.

Manager: Why?

*Raynham, Massachusetts*

## He Placed Out of the Class Where You Learn Not to Be a Jerk

Boss: Hey, do you think you could go down to the cafeteria and get me one of those teeny tiny things of 1 percent milk for my cereal?

Intern: You know, with my dual degree from business school I think I may be able to swing that. . . . I'll bring another intern as backup just in case.

*555 Madison Avenue, New York, New York*

## Remind Me Again Why You're in Charge?

Employee #1: Do we have any Band-Aids in the back?

Manager, after long pause: Uh . . . I don't think so.

Employee #2: Oh, Susan* said we did. I need one.

Manager: Um . . . I'm pretty sure we don't, but I'll look.

After disappearing in the back for five minutes, manager comes back out to the register.

Employee #1: So, there were none back there?

Manager: Nope.

Employee #2: I'm sure there are some. Not even in the first-aid kit?

Manager, after another long pause: Ohhh! Band-Aids! I thought you said, "Mayonnaise"!

*Victoria's Secret, New Mexico*

bosses

## He Said I Was Cold and Unfeeling and Made Abrupt Transitions

Boss: Sorry about being slow with the orders this summer. I was depressed and almost left my husband. Moving on, I have now ordered some new backpacks for us to sell.

*North Washington Avenue, Scranton, Pennsylvania*

## Working in the Magic 8-Ball Factory

Executive: Is it okay if I take the intern with me to the meeting tomorrow?
Assistant: Sure.
Executive: Are you the person I ask about that?
Assistant: No.

*Los Angeles, California*

## Oh! If I'd Known I Would've Brought My Brain

Vice president: Hi! Nice to see you. I hope we'll be meeting soon!
Ad agency rep: Yes—like right now? Since that's why we're here.

*Central Park South, New York, New York*

## But a 99 Percent Chance It Will Be Stupid

Director: For your baby shower, are people buying pink or blue?

Vice president: Blue. Doctor says there's a 50 percent chance it will be a boy.

*San Fernando Boulevard, San Jose, California*

## When Your Job Is Over Hard

Waitress: Can I ask you something? This customer wants two eggs, but he wants them fried. Do we even do that here?
Manager: Um, yes. Actually, most eggs are fried. There's over easy, sunny-side-up, over hard . . .
Waitress: Oh, really? Okay. Whatever.

*30th & Walnut Streets, Boulder, Colorado*

## Why Rome Fell

Employee on phone: My buddy just told me this story about how his wife was so drunk last weekend in a high-end club in the Hamptons and she ran to the bathroom to puke but never fully made it to the toilet. On top of that, as she was puking everywhere, turns out she was also shitting herself. So now the whole club had to be closed down because it smelled like shit and puke. Isn't that hysterical?

Boss walks in.

Employee to boss: Hey, do you know this club?
Boss: Yeah. I actually went there last Saturday night, but we left immediately because it smelled like shit and vomit.

*60th Street & Madison Avenue, New York, New York*

## In Practice, the Principle of Universal Brotherhood Causes Nothing but Confusion

Supervisor: So, you and your brother have different fathers, then?
Worker: Yeah.
Supervisor: So you guys are related through your mom. . . .
Worker: Nah, not really.
Supervisor: Wait, so how are you guys related, then?
Worker: I don't know. We're just brothers.

*3901 Via Oro Avenue, Long Beach, California*

## Sometimes on the Highway He Just Lets Go of the Wheel

Boss: I'm just going to stop taking notes and just use yours after the meeting, because I have no idea what's going on.

*545 5th Avenue, New York, New York*

## Do You Think You'll Be Happy Working for a Non-Prophet Organization?

Boss: So, you're Muslim, right?
Newbie: Yup.
Boss: So you're from the country of Islam?
Newbie: No, not quite.

*Houston, Texas*

## Now Here Are Some Condoms and a Hole Punch . . .

Chief financial officer: Our budget has been balanced the last few years because of unpaid maternity leaves, and we are working that into our models for coming years.

Committee member: So our financial solvency is based on people in the company having sex?

Chief financial officer: Basically.

*Klaipeda, Lithuania*


## But Not *While* Practicing—We've Had Very Mixed Results with That

Account manager on phone: How can she be a virgin? She's a doctor! Would you want your doctor to be a virgin? I think by law you should have to have sex before you are able to practice medicine.

*171 Nepean Street, Ottawa, Ontario, Canada*


## Sure, Emperor. Sure.

Boss: Just because I don't wear my clothes to work doesn't mean I don't have them.

*55 Elk Street, Albany, New York*

bosses

## Eventually, Sure

Manager #1: So, did you have a nice birthday party?

Manager #2: Not yet. My older brother's birthday is two weeks after mine, so we always just have one big party that weekend.

Manager #1: Oh, wait—wouldn't that make you the older brother?

*3043 Glendale Avenue, Toledo, Ohio*

## Well, It's Like I Always Say: Children Come First

Male bank president: My daughter's gonna letter in high school track this year.

Female vice president: Oh?

Male bank president: Yeah, she's a runner. All year I've been taking her out on country roads to let her spread her legs.

Female vice president, under her breath: Putz!

*1105 Vargas Street, Atwood, Kansas*

## This Is Your Brain on Market Research

Advertising executive: Here are my recommendations: (A) Can we simplify this? (B) Consumers are stupid.

*Chicago, Illinois*

## Dog: Sweetie, All You Have to Do Is Say, "Please"

Chairman: It will be easy—like pulling a greasy stick out a dog's arse.

Employee: That's all well and good, but we have to get the greasy stick in there first!

*Cumbria, England*


## Her Résumé Comes with a Centerfold

Boss: Did you talk to that girl, Rachel*?
Male employee on phone: Yes, I have her résumé in front of me now.
Boss: She's very pretty . . . She has big boobs.
Male employee on phone: Really?
Boss: Something to think about.

*6671 Eastland Road, Cleveland, Ohio*


## Why Not Everyone Should Reproduce

Waiter at new copy machine: Which way does this go in, facedown or -up, sideways or lengthways? You're not going to tell me, are you?
Manager: We've got plenty of paper over there. Keep trying until you get it right.

*45 South Illinois Street, Indianapolis, Indiana*


## Just Another Typical Day Here at the Department of Redundancy Department

Manager: What was the soup du jour of the day today?

*Sterling Forest Road, Sterling Forest, New York*

bosses

## Meeting at NewKink Development Corporation

Manager: So, can we finally take his picture off the home page?

Developer: What's the matter? Do you have something against nipples?

Manager: I don't even like the word *nipples*. . . . *Butter*— that's another word I don't like.

Developer: You should meet a friend of mine. She doesn't like the word *goggles*.

*Centre Street, New York, New York*

## First the Briefing, Then the Stabbing

Supervisor: So, Tina* and I are actually getting along really well! We discovered that we both have the same work style, which is Crazy Psycho Bitch.

*473 Ridge Road, Dayton, New Jersey*

## Michael Milken's Up to His Old Tricks

Exec steals Nutri-Grain Bar from CEO.

CEO: Give that back!

Exec: No.

CEO, pushing exec against the wall: Give that to me—that's my Nutri-Grain!

Exec: You aren't getting it back.

CEO: That's stealing, man!

Exec: Buy some more! You've got the money!

CEO, releasing exec: You're a real class act, man.

Exec unwraps and eats Nutri-Grain Bar.

*5200 Dixie Road, Toronto, Ontario, Canada*

## Natural Selection Fires Off a Warning Shot

Manager: Ow. Shit. Shit. Fuck. Shit!
Peon: What's wrong?
Manager: I accidentally ironed my arm this morning, and
now it hurts every time I touch anything with it.

*1180 Jefferson Road, Rochester, New York*

## A Recent Graduate of Turnip Truck University

Employee: I'd like to work the booth. I could be good at that.
I'd like to travel and go to trade shows.
Manager: You'd have to educate yourself so you can speak
to clients about what we do here. You'd also have to
work some weekends.
Employee: Do I get paid?
Manager: You get travel for free—meals, hotel, airfare.
Employee: Wow.
Manager: And, of course, your regular paycheck.
Employee: Is this scheme widely known in the company?

*Rochelle Park, New Jersey*

## I Will Need Additional Information to Arrive at a Decision

Exec: I'll be right back, so don't lock me out.

Cleaning lady: If I knew who the hell you were, maybe I'd consider it.

Exec: I'm the reason you have a job.

*725 East 40th Street, Holland, Michigan*


## Had to Wait for the Firewall to Stop Smoking

Boss: Do we have Google installed on our Internet?

IT guy: We put it on your machine yesterday.

*700 West Van Buren Street, Chicago, Illinois*


## By the Way, We Need More Magazines in the Men's Room

Boss: So, is there any other duty that you do on a daily basis that we should include on this list?

Worker: You mean, other than miscellaneous bullshit?

Boss: Well, how much time do you spend on miscellaneous bullshit every day?

Worker: Depending on the day, between ten minutes and eight hours.

*4913 West Laurel Street, Tampa, Florida*

## We Need a Quorum to Get High

Vice president to another: Now all we need is a bong and
multiple partners!

*37th Street & 7th Avenue, New York, New York*

## . . . But I've Got to Pay the Coke Bill, So Gimme
## Fifty Bucks and We'll Snuggle

Supervisor: So I said to my son, "You want me to cuddle
with you?" And he said, "No, Daddy, I've already slept
with enough people today."

*473 Ridge Road, Dayton, New Jersey*

## Well, an IV, Some Sort of Modified Reciprocal Saw,
## a Rubber Hand, and a Lot of Lotion Ought to Do
## the Trick

General manager: Listen, if you guys can find a way for me
to whack off another six months, that would be great.

*115th Avenue Northeast, Kirkland, Washington*

## Bill Clinton Was a Better President Than He Is a
## Campaign Manager

Boss: We never decided to postpone this issue. We just
agreed that we would deal with other issues first.

*Brouwersvliet, Antwerp, Belgium*

## You Have to Keep One Eye on Them at All Times

Supervisor surfing the Net: Look! A Cyclops baby was born in India! This is what happens when I don't keep up with current events!

*666 5th Avenue, New York, New York*

## And I'll Say, "Harder, Slave"

Employee: It seems like there are a lot of new people working here.

Boss: Yes . . . Sometimes I'll be leaving the building and will say to someone, "I don't know you," and they will say, "I work for you."

*Elevator, 215 Michigan Avenue, Chicago, Illinois*

## Why Don't You Give It a Try and We'll See?

Manager to underling: Haven't apes evolved to the point where they could do your job?

*3888 Stewart Road, Eugene, Oregon*

## He'd Rather Do It Avocationally

Manager: Why do they send so much of this stock? It's never gonna sell. What bunch of arseholes thought this up at head office?

Peon: This is really getting to you, isn't it? I get the feeling you applied for a job there and they turned you down.

Manager: A job at head office? No, thanks. I've no desire to be an arsehole for a living.
Peon: But you'd be so good at it.

*Lincoln, England*


## How's Tomorrow Sound?

Underling: What do you want me to do today?
Superboss: That's a good question. I can talk about that whenever you're ready.

*4000 Shoreline Court, San Francisco, California*


## Well, You and I Could Still Meet

Manager: So, the meeting is cancelled.
Office hoochie: And I put a clean thong on for this!

*1950 Broadway, Oakland, California*


## He Believes Chrysler Daimlered for Our Sins

Boss on phone: What religion is he? . . . That makes sense that he drives a Jeep, then.

*Northbrook, Illinois*


## What Would Jesus Eat?

Manager: You know, people a long time ago—people like Jesus—they weren't fat.

*2904 Rodeo Park Drive East, Santa Fe, New Mexico*

## From *The Complete Idiot's Guide to Business Diplomacy*

Exec forwarding an email to whole company: I don't know if any of you have seen this summary. You may find it a useful "Idiot's Guide."

Employee: Are you implying everyone you just sent this to is an idiot?

Exec: Not in the slightest! I was implying the guy who sent it to me thought I was an idiot.

*1251 Avenue of the Americas, New York, New York*

## How to Tell If Your Coworker Is Actually a Robot

Male exec: I won't be able to be at the pitch—my grand-father died.

Female exec: Oh my god, I'm so sorry.

Male exec: It's okay. I still have my other grandfather.

Female exec: That's why you have two children, right? If one of them dies, you've still got the other one so it's not so sad.

*Film studio, 100 Universal Plaza, Universal City, California*

## Mine Is to Lose Them

Secretary: I can write memos like it's my job.

Boss: That *is* your job.

*100 East Rivercenter Boulevard, Covington, Kentucky*

## She Must Be Lonely Among Her Kind

Supervisor to employee: I'm sorry, I don't speak Retard.

*588 North Gulph Road, King of Prussia, Pennsylvania*

## Empiricist Cooking Has Its Limitations

Vice president: But how will we make grilled cheese?

Drone: With the toaster oven.

Vice president: Well, I never . . . You'll have to show me how to use it.

Drone: Have you used a toaster?

Vice president: Yes!

Drone: Have you used an oven?

Vice president: *Yes!*

Drone: Then you can use a toaster oven.

Vice president: Well, I have never seen such a thing.

*Benzing Road, Orchard Park, New York*

## He Does Love His Wife's Butt

Branch manager on phone: Hello? Okay, put him through. Hey, Matt\*! Hold on, let me shut my office door. . . . Yeah . . . Yeah . . . I do love my wife . . .

Cubicle chick: Did he just say what I think he said? "I do love my wife"?

Sales guy: Yes, but I think you missed a part. He said "I do love my wife, *but* . . ."

Cubicle chick: It's gonna be a *goood* day!

*8220 England Street, Charlotte, North Carolina*

## Tough Love at the Massage Parlor

Supervisor: Jeremy* did not come in or call for three days. What should we do?

Manager: Spank him?

*803 West Seale Street, Nacogdoches, Texas*

## All I Want Is a Hand-Turkey for Thanksgiving. What Do I Get? Two Lousy Short Stories about Pilgrims!

Manager #1: My kids *suck* at arts and crafts.

Manager #2: No glitter? No glue? No macaroni or Popsicle sticks?

Manager #1: Holy shit, no. They are the epitome of suck.

*West Irving Park Road, Roselle, Illinois*

## The "Advanced" Section of the *Kama Sutra* Is Not for Everyone

Manager: Yeah, in order for me to work it out I had to bend over backwards and slap some KY jelly on it.

*Electronics store, California*

## . . . Or I'm Constipated

Assistant: Are you going to be in next week?

Vice president: Yes . . . Unless al-Qaeda does something.

*1120 20th Street NW, Washington, DC*

## Because Their Secretary Told Me They're Missing Page 47 Over There

Boss: I've got part of the *Kama Sutra* on my wall.
Employee: Do we need to talk to HR?

*175 South 3rd Street, Columbus, Ohio*


## Because, After This Conversation, I May Need to Blow My Brains Out

Boss: How was your day?
Employee miming pointing a gun to his head: Know what I mean? But it's over now.
Boss: My father killed himself six months ago.
Employee: Did he use a gun?

*47 Catherwood Road, Ithaca, New York*


## Okay, People, You Are to Cease Using the Austin Powers Films in Management Training

Underling: Is that what you need?
Boss: I was asking for a shark with laser beams, and I got a manatee with flashlights? Thanks.

*Kadena Air Base, Okinawa, Japan*


## Well, You'll Have Lots of Time to Practice, Because You're Fired

Supervisor: Did someone order colored pencils from the office supply place?

bosses

33

Assistant: I'm thinking of becoming a caricaturist.

*330 Madison Avenue, New York, New York*

## Just Long Enough to Use the Word *Fuck*

Area manager: We will need to open an investigation into this and see what happened.

Superintendent: I'll tell you what happened—he fucked up!

Area manager: Well, I didn't say it needed to be a *long* investigation.

*128 Spring Street, Ypsilanti, Michigan*

## Performance Review Time at the CIA

General manager: I told you to respect your boss—I didn't tell you to obey her orders.

*230 North College Street, Charlotte, North Carolina*

## It's Hard Out There for a Da Vinci

Boss: By the way, I changed a lot of your code, so if it breaks, that's why.

*5720 Green Circle Drive, Minnetonka, Minnesota*

## You Can Feel the Silent Pressure of Her Presence on the Line, Though

Supervisor: She always answers the phone. It's just . . . she forgets to talk.

*200 West Oak Street, Fort Collins, Colorado*

## Okay. How Often Do You Visit the Men's Room, Then?

Department head: So, can we update your job description tomorrow morning?

Employee: No, I have a color correction session to attend.

Department head: Well, I notice you don't take lunch. You're usually at your desk. What about then?

Employee: I do take lunch. I just eat at my desk and read a book or something.

Department head: Well, how about doing something more productive with that time? Do you want to meet then?

Employee: No.

*6423 Wilshire Boulevard, Los Angeles, California*


## He Means He Wants the Final Text Written on Papyrus

Boss: I don't need to see everything before it goes out the door. Just send me a final, final rough draft.

*Union Square, New York, New York*


## When Yuppies Claim Workers' Comp

Manager preparing staff party: Oh my god, look! I cut so much cheese I got a blister!

*City Centre Building, Ottawa, Ontario, Canada*

bosses

35

## Why Night Guy Volunteered to Work Nights

Boss: Why didn't you build those three displays last night?

Night guy: I couldn't find the stuff to do it with.

Boss, going back and pointing to three pallets of stuff in back room: This is the stuff you couldn't find all night?

Night guy: You should have put in my note that I should look harder.

*Salt Lake City, Utah*

## He's a Ninja

Boss to client and client's son: So, this is your youngest boy, isn't it? I've met him before.

Client: Uh, I don't think you have.

Boss: Yeah, I'm sure I have. . . . He's Down's syndrome, isn't he?

Client: No.

*98 Fitzroy Street, Grafton, Australia*

## Well, Some of the Time, Anyway

Office manager: We kinda have a policy we sorta have to follow.

*5757 Wilshire Boulevard, Los Angeles, California*

## Her Oonication Skills Need Work

Associate: Hey, can you come look at my pooter?

Manager: Your what?

Associate: What? . . . *What?* Come on, my com*puter*!

*Mass Street, Lawrence, Kansas*

## Defining Expectations

Office manager: The first rule of thumb is that two geotechnical engineers will always give you two different answers. The second rule of thumb is that I'm always right.

Interns: Hahahaha.

Office manager, after long pause: I'm being serious.

*1066 West Hastings Street, Vancouver,
British Columbia, Canada*

## I'm Almost Positive You Have to Have an IQ of at Least 30 to Qualify As a Member of the Human Race

Boss: Where did he live? Are you attending the funeral?

Employee: He lived in Alaska. No. Unfortunately, I won't be able to attend the funeral.

Boss: Why?

Employee: Well, I have to double-check with Human Resources, but I'm almost positive the person has to die in the United States for you to qualify for the three-day leave.

*Supervisor's office, Washington, DC*

## Which Is Bad for the Jell-O

Sales manager: Man, I wish it would quit raining. My swimming pool's getting full of water.

*Dover Road, Clarksville, Tennessee*

bosses

## In Our Business There's Nothing Like the Personal Touch

Manager: Well, I'm still hoping I can do him manually. Wait, that didn't sound right, did it?

*Atlanta, Georgia*

## I Can't Answer You Without Breaking the Law

Boss: Come over here. What is an over-the-top chick flick?
Longtime admin lady: *Ghost.*
Boss: No.
Longtime admin lady: What kind of chick flick do you want?
Boss: How about *Vagina Monologues*?
Longtime admin lady: How is that a chick flick?

*Madison, Wisconsin*

## This Midlife Crisis Is Coming Together Nicely

CEO: I hit a garbage truck this morning!
Admin: What?
CEO: I hit a garbage truck this morning! Broadsided it! Never even saw it!
Admin: You didn't see a garbage truck?
CEO: I know! I was doing, like, forty miles an hour! And my kid was in the car!

*1190 Del Rio Place, Ontario, Canada*

## Also, That Sandwich Is Too Big

Manager: I'll take the eight-inch. Twelve inches may be a little too much.

*Columbia, Maryland*


## The Hairy Palms and Blindness Are Worth It

Supervisor at morning break piñata event: If we whack it hard enough the goodies will come out of it!

*1615 Bluff City Highway, Bristol, Tennessee*


## A Judicious Sprinkling of Fairy Dust Should Suffice

Manager: Oh my god! I can't *believe* I forgot to take my magic wand to the meeting!

*1000 Capital of Texas Highway, Austin, Texas*


## Ladies, Your Dreams Have Come True

Boss: What's in my butt?! What's in my butt?! *What's in my butt?!* [Reaches into pants and pulls out cell phone clip.] Oh, this must've come out when I went pee.

*2800 Via Cabrillo Marina, San Pedro, California*

## Have Kneepads. Will Take Dictation.

Manager: Well, let's get you a chair.

Receptionist: Oh, that's okay. I can go on my knees. I really just need to watch you do it.

*100 Heritage Reserve, Menomonee Falls, Wisconsin*

## I'm a Mr. Sketch "Lemon" Aficionado, Myself

Secretary #1: Close up that marker—the smell makes me ill.

Boss: I like the way they smell. [Waves it around.]

Secretary #1: Seriously, it makes me sick.

Secretary #2: I like it, too. I like the big thick ones the best, though.

*Allen Park, Michigan*

## How Do You Run Bent Over Like That?

Supervisor to employee: Look at you scurry away! It looks like your mouth is full of nuts!

*4425 Steele Lane, Santa Rosa, California*

## Good-bye, Mr. Clips

Manager: Only forty more days till I leave. . . .

Assistant: Oh, damn!

Manager: Don't be so upset—it's still a little while away, yet. . . .

Assistant: Oh, that's sad, too, but I just broke my favorite clip. It's disappointing. I love these clips. . . .

*1111 Amsterdam Avenue, New York, New York*

## Joined the Undead?

CEO: The only living relative I have left died last year!

*Austin, Texas*

## That's Not Usually a Concession

General manager: I'm no Forrest Gump, but I'm pretty good.

*Franklin & Lyndale Avenues, Minneapolis, Minnesota*

## And If You Get It Right Up It'll Stay Upright . . . and Still Kill People

Senior engineer to intern: If you get it wrong it'll collapse and kill people.

*1066 West Hastings, Vancouver, British Columbia, Canada*

## I Don't. Take Off Your Pants.

Account manager: How do you know I'm a girl?

*214 West 39th Street, New York, New York*

## November: You'll Be Thankful When It's Over!

Sales rep: We need a way to describe November.
Sales manager: Cold and shitty.

*Lower Westfield Road, Holyoke, Massachusetts*

## Then Middle Earth

District manager: Yeah, we're going on a Mediterranean cruise. We fly in to Rome and then we go to Paris, then France, then Norway. . . .

*King Street, Toronto, Ontario, Canada*

# ((coworkers

## A Help Desk Instant Classic

Girl: It said my cookies aren't turned on. What am I supposed to do, pour some milk on myself and show them
my tits?

*234 West 42nd Street, New York, New York*


## But When I Called It Out in Bed?

Coworker #1: Did you happen to grab my printouts, Jason?
[Long pause, then] Did you see anything here?
Coworker #2: No.
Coworker #1: Is this yours? No? It says, "Jason Palmer."*
Coworker #2: My name's not Jason. It's Tom.*
Coworker #1: Why haven't you ever corrected me?
Coworker #2, shrugging: You just always called me Jason.

*3814 Walnut Street, Philadelphia, Pennsylvania*


## Faith-Based Employee Assistance Program

Upset worker: Oh, Lord! Jesus! Jesus! *Jesus!* Lord, help me!
Voice from speakerphone: You called?

*8900 Northwest 35th Lane, Miami, Florida*


## Local Sports Editor Arrested by Karma Police, Sentenced to Ride "It's a Small World" in Perpetuity

City editor: Do you think they give you your money back if
your kid dies at Disney World?

Editor in Chief: No, but Mickey Mouse volunteers to be a pallbearer at the funeral.

Sports editor, in a Mickey Mouse falsetto: Hey guys, what's in the box?

*7 North Jefferson Street, Huntington, Indiana*

## How About, "Don't You Wish Your Savior Was Hot Like Me?"

Blocked writer: Do you know how hard it is to write a useful, *edifying* sermon when you've got "Don't you wish your girlfriend was hot like me" stuck in your head?

*1701 Delancey Street, Philadelphia, Pennsylvania*

## Someone Better Rife This Guy Before He Causes Any Serious Madage

Admin: I just ordered the pizzas, but I don't know if it's gonna get here. I kept telling them, "Our building is on Exalander Road," and they didn't even know where that was.

Boss: We work on Alexander Road.

Admin: I know, that's what I kept telling them—Exalander Road—but they had no clue.

*Route 1 South & Alexander Road, Princeton, New Jersey*

## I Still Have Trouble Believing in Star Jones!

Lady office grunt: One of my colleagues just began a sentence with, "Star Jones says . . ." *I can't fucking believe I work here!*

*Oxnard Street, Los Angeles, California*

## Nah, Turns Out It Was Just a Life Insurance Scam

Peon #1: I just read that there has been a 104 percent increase in the numbers of lost or stolen cows recovered in Texas and Oklahoma.

Peon #2: So they found four more cows than were actually lost?

*650 California Street, San Francisco, California*

## Your Testimony Is Highly Suspect

Designer: Here, just try it.

Writer: No.

Designer: Come on! Why are you being so stubborn?

Writer, shouting: I am not putting that in my mouth! It's all limp! [Pause, then shouting into hallway] I was talking about *French fries*!

*16340 North Scottsdale Road, Scottsdale, Arizona*

## He Already Has Plans for Them

Employee #1: Dave,* you're what, twenty-seven? You're too young to get married. You need to wait until you're thirty-five and then marry a twenty-three-year-old. Birthing is just Bam! Bam! Bam!—brutal on them. . . . So you need to marry young.

Employee #2: So I need to work here for eight years and marry a girl who is just graduating from here?

Employee #3: Start looking, man. She's in high school now.

Employee #2: She'd be what, fifteen? Hey, Jim,* how old are your daughters?

Employee #1: Thirteen and fifteen . . . *Shut up!*

*3800 Victory Parkway, Cincinnati, Ohio*


## Rule of Thumb: Don't Hire Anyone Who Has Ever Performed a *Mortal Kombat* Move in Real Life

Applicant explaining multiyear gap in employment history: I got sent to jail for stabbing a guy twelve times, but it was bullshit.

Manager: Oh, yeah?

Applicant: Yeah. I only stabbed him six times; I just had two knives in my hand. It was bullshit.

Manager: Hmmm. I see.

*Indianapolis, Indiana*


## He's Fated to *Become* the Regional Manager

Employee: Fuck you very much for calling Popular Video Store.* How may I abuse you? . . . Oh, hi, Bill* [regional manager] . . . Yeah, today's my last day.

*Video store, Del Mar, California*

## Actually, He's Just Hung Like a Bull Moose, and Word Gets Around

Attorney #1: You know Barry,* the blind prosecutor down-
town?

Attorney #2: He's the one who always gets the young, hot
assistants, right?

Attorney #3: I don't care what anyone says, that son of a
bitch can see.

*300 West Main Street, Louisville, Kentucky*

## It's Amazing He Can Be Such a Good Lawyer, Despite Being Blind

Female staffer #1: You know what Donald* said to me? He
said, "In case you know anyone who's having a vasectomy, I have some advice for you to give them." And then
he told me about how they gave him a jockstrap to wear
after his surgery to keep everything in place, but that the
one they gave him was too small. And I said, "Donald! I
don't want to hear any more!" But he kept talking about
how uncomfortable it was to wear a jockstrap that was
too small for him after having his vasectomy. I was afraid
he was going to start describing exactly how his balls
were getting squeezed.

Female staffer #2: See, that's a perfect example of how
Donald is always so passive. If he weren't so passive,
he'd just say, "I want everyone to know I'm hung like a
horse."

*10 Medical Center Boulevard, Winston-Salem, North Carolina*

## And He Won't Be. Until the Next Time.

Coworker whispering on phone: And I know I've said this before, but I will *never* be naked in the file room again. . . .

*2811 Wilshire Boulevard, Santa Monica, California*

## Rob Schneider? Is That You?

Customer: Can you draw something on the cake for me?
Employee: Sure, what do you want on it?
Customer: A dick.
Employee: I can do you one better. We've got these chocolate-covered bananas and chocolate-covered cookie-dough balls. I can put an edible, chocolate-covered dick and balls on your cake.
Customer: Fucking awesome!
Manager, walking in: Uh, what are you doing?
Employee: Making a dick cake.
Manager: Woo! Makin' a dick cake!

*Ice-cream store, East Village, New York, New York*

## Yep, PDAs Are Definitely What's Going to Precipitate the Second Coming

Old black lady worker to young couple kissing and groping: What the hell is wrong with these peoples? Jesus needs to come down and knock some damn sense into their stupid motherfucking ass.

*Power company, Las Vegas, Nevada*

## The Personal Is Political

Lady coworker #1: Your boss asked you to be sure to attend the company party at a strip club?!

Lady coworker #2: Yeah, what's so bad about that?

Lady coworker #1: Well, you're going to be surrounded by naked, gyrating ladies, and that's sexist and outrageous!

Lady coworker #2: Really? I was looking forward to seeing my sister.

*630 East Lake Street, Chicago, Illinois*

## If the Goal Is to Go Home at Five, Then You're on the Right Track

Employee: Someone just called me. They said, "Hello," and asked if I could help them because they had a question. I didn't know what to do so I said, "No," and hung up. Was that okay?

Boss: I guess that's one way of handling it.

*Patent and Trademark Office, Alexandria, Virginia*

## So, Similar to Washing Down a Whole Bottle of Tylenol with a Fifth of Jack Daniel's

IT nerd #1: Well, it's kinda like when you are on 'shrooms.

IT nerd #2: Um . . .

IT nerd #1: Okay, well, same thing as LSD.

IT nerd #2: I have never tried that, either.

IT nerd #1: Peyote?

IT nerd #2: No . . .

IT nerd #1: Mescaline?

IT nerd #2: I have never tried illegal drugs.

IT nerd #1: Okay, well, it's kinda like quickly drinking eight or nine bottles of NyQuil.

IT nerd #2: *Ohhh*, okay. That I've done. Now I understand.

*Tokyo, Japan*

## Why I Have No Pictures on My Desk

Lackey: So, that's your wife, huh?

Suit: Yep.

Lackey: She's a grade-school teacher?

Suit: Yes.

Lackey: She looks like that one that had sex with her thirteen-year-old student.

*275 West Wisconsin Avenue, Milwaukee, Wisconsin*

## And I Wrote It in the Funbag Programming Language

Engineer #1: What the hell were you thinking when you wrote this code?

Engineer #2: Boobs.

Engineer #1: Huh?!

Engineer #2: Truthfully, it's likely I was thinking about boobs.

*Columbia, Maryland*

## The Government *Is* Watching Him, but Only for Laughs

Clerk guy: Yeah, so we ordered a pizza last night, and the guy on the phone knew my address—get this—before I even told him!

Clerk girl: Don't they have caller ID or something?

Clerk guy: Man, I don't know. I was smoking a big one, and I was like, "Dude, whoa. I think the government is all watching me now."

Clerk girl: Um, probably not.

Clerk guy: Then explain to me how they knew my address *and* what kind of pizza I ordered last time! Explain that!

*Temple, Texas*

## You'll Be Surprised and You Won't Even Know It!

Employee: I'm totally gonna sneak up on you when you're not here.

*575 5th Avenue, New York, New York*

## And the Smell of Pending Litigation

Electrician: I think I may have made a mistake.

Office owner: Ya think so? What gave it away, the flames?

*528 Newtown Road, Virginia Beach, Virginia*

## Here, I'll Show You with My Fingers—the Difference Is the Long One in the Middle

Senior consultant: Hey, what's the difference between four and five?

Consultant: How am I getting paid less than you?

*Waterloo, London, England*


## Nah, the Saddle's Just for This Guy I Sometimes Torture Sexually

Female admin: What were you doing here at 7:40?

Male admin: I was rummaging through your stuff.

Female admin: Find anything of interest? My stuff is pretty boring.

Male admin: Really? I found that riding crop quite interesting.

Female admin: What? I ride horses!

Male admin: That would explain the saddle.

*80 Grasslands Road, Elmsford, New York*


## I Think the Motherboard Is Pregnant

Suit: Help desk? My computer went down on me.

Tech support: Please hold on. [Turns on speakerphone.] Can you repeat that?

Suit: My computer went down on me!

Tech support, with entire support team laughing in the background: So, what's the problem?

*2nd Street, Jersey City, New Jersey*

coworkers

53

## You're Fired

Woman #1: I don't think I can handle a two-hour meeting.
Woman #2: The trick is to doodle in your notebook the whole time—it looks like you're taking notes.
Woman #1: I can design outfits for my cat rodeo!

*330 South 3rd Street, Minneapolis, Minnesota*

## This Could Explain Why Her Teeth Chipped Yesterday Morning

Lady worker #1: Oh, look at the pretty rock!
Lady worker #2: Um . . . That's part of a blueberry muffin.
Lady worker #1: Oh.

*Monument Circle, Indianapolis, Indiana*

## My Brain Is Still in Its Original Wrapping

Employee: So, we were going to mail all these invoices, but instead we're going to fax them since our postage machine died. Just put them on here and press Start.
Temp: Okay! Got it. [Begins faxing.]
Employee: Um, you have to take them out of the envelopes first.

*380 Interlocken Crescent Boulevard, Broomfield, Colorado*

## But I Play One on TV

M.D. #1: Hey, look! They named their kid *Babygirl*!
M.D. #2: No way, that's hilarious!

Janitor: Actually, it just means they haven't named their child yet, and that it's a baby girl.

M.D. #1: Are you a doctor?

M.D. #2: I bet he's not even a doctor.

Janitor: [Walks away.]

*Hospital, Lacey, Washington*


## Why IT Dude Is Regularly Beaten Up

Deputy: There was a wreck this weekend where a guy hit a tree at sixty miles per hour—ripped off the right side of his head. You could actually see inside his skull. We never could find his brain, though.

Project manager: Did it kill him?

IT dude: Nope, he is walking around managing projects.

*U.S. Highway 69/75, Oklahoma*


## Or Tommy Lee

Female employee #1: So, if the sun exploded seven minutes ago we wouldn't know it yet, because it takes eight minutes for the sun's light to reach us.

Male employee: That's depressing! What would you do in those seven minutes?

Female employee #1: If I were at work? Have sex.

Male employee: Isn't that a lot of pressure on the guy?

Female employee #1: Please. Guys are usually all, "Gimme two minutes!"

Female employee #2: You could do three guys in that time!

Female employee #1: Three and a half!

*Boulevard Sacré-Coeur, Gatineau, Quebec, Canada*

## We Call Them "Rotational Assignments," and You Would Get a Special Chair

Interviewer #1: You have had many jobs at that same company. Can you describe your work environment?

Forty-six-year-old proper woman: My company liked to move us around a lot, so we got experience in different departments.

Interviewer #1: Was this a standard practice?

Forty-six-year-old proper woman: Oh, yes. They did that for everyone working at the restaurant's HQ. Every six months we would move from department to department. We liked to call it "tossing the salad."

Interviewer #1: Excuse me?

Interviewer #2: [Spits out his water.]

Interviewers #3, #4, and #5: [Look away and giggle uncontrollably.]

Forty-six-year-old proper woman: I got my salad tossed every six months but in the past year moved it up to every three months. It's all part of the manager training program.

Interviewer #6: Did you like getting your salad tossed?

Forty-six-year-old proper woman: Yes, I did.

Interviewer #6: It must take some getting used to. We have never tossed salads here, but that is not to say we won't someday.

Forty-six-year-old proper woman: I would highly recommend it.

*Church Street, Orlando, Florida*


## I Can't Wait to See That "Help Wanted" Ad

Lesbian worker: Whatever it takes to get her pregnant . . . Even if I have to participate!

*1250 Broadway, New York, New York*


## In the Future, Black People Will Get to Do Things While Whitey Pays to Watch

Black coworker: Hey, how are you doing today?

Redneck coworker: If I were you I wouldn't speak to me today.

Black coworker: Why is that? What's wrong with you?

Redneck coworker: I'm not too fond of you black people today. That damn Tiger Woods has won another Major.

Black coworker: Oh, that's all? Well, what are you going to do when we take over NASCAR?

Redneck coworker: [Bewildered silence.]

*1000 Jerry Saint Pé Highway, Mississippi*


## Once You Hear the Phrase "Tore My Ass Muscle," the Worst Is Almost Certainly Over

Female employee: Are you limping?

Male employee: Yeah, I tore my ass muscle again.

Female admin: Just stop right there, I don't want to hear any more.

*84 Newbury Street, Peabody, Massachusetts*

## This Conversation Has Gone Balls-Up

British employee: Well, this was supposed to be completed by now. It looks like it's gone all cock-up.

American #1: What?

British employee: I'm sorry, do you not have that phrase here?

American #2: In America you can't say "cock" like that. I shouldn't hear you say "cock."

American #1: We say "fuck." Fucked up.

British employee: Okay, how's this: Fuck off.

*1 Corporate Drive, Orangeburg, New York*

## But Aren't We Scheduled to Exchange Briefs and Deliver Oral Arguments?

Office Assistant: If I go back to the phone without an answer this guy is going to eat me out.

Manager: I think you mean *chew* you out.

*1125 Colonel Drive, Ottawa, Ontario, Canada*

## His Desk Plate Says, "I'd Rather Be Blistered"

Office peon #1: Give me a break! I've been here since 6 a.m.!

Office peon #2: Why would you do that to yourself?

Office peon #1: Well, I've been a very bad boy, and I deserve a spanking. But that's too expensive here in the city, so instead I do this.

*469 7th Avenue, New York, New York*

## Look Who's Talking, Dr. Vah-jay-jay

Male nurse #1: I just thought of something—wouldn't it be so embarrassing being a gynecologist? What's your motivation? Man, that would just be *so* embarrassing.

Male nurse #2: Yeah, especially with your name: Dr. Beaver.

*Medical Center, Danville, Pennsylvania*

## Can't Wait till He Puts on the Darth Vader Mask and Tells the Baby He's Her Father

Woman #1: Hey, look at you! I didn't know you were back from maternity leave.

Woman #2: Yeah, I just came back yesterday.

Woman #1: I saw the pictures you emailed. She's adorable. I remember you were worried about labor. How'd it go?

Woman #2: Not too bad, actually. Kind of what I expected . . . although I punched my husband and threatened divorce during the worst of it.

Woman #1: Are you serious? What did he do?

Woman #2: Right when my contractions were about two minutes apart he got nervous and attempted to distract me. So he kept making that "oooh-bah, oooh-bah" noise that those robot things made in *Revenge of the Sith.*

Woman #1: Oh my god! I know what you're talking about. What a jerk! That's so funny, though.

Woman #2: Yeah, I know. We laugh about it now, but at the time I punched him in the stomach and called him a bastard. I told him if he opened his mouth again, even to cough, we were getting a divorce. Poor guy wouldn't even talk to the nurses after that.

*777 Eisenhower Parkway, Ann Arbor, Michigan*

### Jobs: Aha! We'll Start Attaching a Kid to the 50GB Models. They'll Sell Like Hotcakes!

IT lady #1: How do you work this thing?

IT guy #1: What is it? An iPod?

IT lady #1: Yeah, I'm trying to restart it, but I don't know how.

IT guy #2: Control, alt, delete!

IT lady #1: Don't any of you have iPods to help me out?

IT guy #3: I'll call my kids.

*Aldgate, London, England*

### It's Been Oolong Time Since I Embarrassed Myself Like That

Agent: Oh, now I remember why I don't usually drink pee— it always makes me have to go to the washroom. . . . [Coworkers laugh hysterically and tease.] Tea. Tea! I meant tea! . . . Fuck you all.

*1616 27th Avenue Northeast, Calgary, Alberta, Canada*

## So White She Doesn't Know What's Happened to the N-word

White salesgirl: Jesus, I just got called a nigger!

Filipino salesgirl: What? On your break?

White salesgirl: Yeah! And by a black person! Homeless—I wouldn't give her money. I'm about as cracker as you get—total whitey. I mean, I'm wearing Banana Republic!

*1900 Broadway, Oakland, California*


## At the Annual Association of Homophobic Lexicographers Banquet

Intern #1: So, is there a difference between hom*o*genous and homo*ge*neous?

Intern #2: Yes, one means "composed of one thing," and the other is, like, a gay Einstein or something.

*Rayburn House Building, Washington, DC*


## Nevada Madam: Sign Here

Woman #1: Sometimes I like doing jobs like this.

Woman #2: Like what?

Woman #1: You know, mindless hand jobs.

*380 Lafayette Road East, St. Paul, Minnesota*

coworkers

## Sometimes He'd Euphorically Do Body-Shots Off of Me and Ned from Accounting

Female coworker: I'm so tired of being alone, but it's impossible to meet any available men here. I should have taken John* up on his offer.

Male coworker: Who?

Female coworker: You know, John Allen.* The guy who was here about eight years ago and got booted, then came back a few years later, then got booted again a couple of years ago.

Male coworker: Oh, he's been booted more times than that! What are *you* talking about?

Female coworker: Didn't I tell you? He came back last fall trying to get reinstated and stopped by to see me. He said he'd been thinking about me. He wanted to know if I was interested in getting together, but I didn't want to get into that so I lied and said I was seeing someone. Now I wonder why I did that.

Male coworker: Maybe because he's a bipolar bisexual alcoholic?

Female coworker: There is that. . . . But I bet he wouldn't have bored me.

*Washington State*

## Otherwise, We Can Only Give You This Hillary Mask and Wish You Godspeed

Employer entering office: President Clinton is downstairs on Wacker Drive, but I think you girls will be safe if you just stay inside.

*150 South Wacker Drive, Chicago, Illinois*


## Dan's Discount Dungeon

Female staffer #1: Yeah, we need to get us a gas-powered hedge trimmer.

Male staffer: Yeah, we have an electric, but it's battery-operated. And the battery only lasts about ten minutes, so it's like extreme speed trimming. We have to get to that bush fast before the battery runs out.

Female staffer #2: Are y'all talking about vibrators?

Male staffer: Uh, well, sort of . . . Except this one has teeth that chop long, skinny things in half.

Female staffer #2: Oooh, kinky! Where'd you get it?

*10 Medical Center Boulevard, Winston-Salem, North Carolina*


## But the Pashmina Goats Are Fine with You Taking That Stuff, Because No Woman Wants a Beard

Employee #1: Yeah, so PETA has helped me understand the cruelty animals are subjected to by humans.

Employee #2: I've seen some of the videos. Heinous.

Employee #1: Like that shirt you're wearing—it's made of cotton, right? You shouldn't be wearing it.

coworkers

Employee #2: Huh? Why not?
Employee #1: It really hurts the sheep when they are shorn.
*Home supplies store, Cape Cod, Massachusetts*

## Way-Too-Casual Friday

Coworker #1: I have to go expose myself to Bob* and Mike*
in a meeting now.
Coworker #2: Maybe I should skip that meeting.
*1701 North Collins Boulevard, Richardson, Texas*

## You, for Example, Should Forget It

Salesguy #1: . . . So she totally doesn't mind sexual harassment.
Salesguy #2: Really?
Salesguy #1: Well, she does and she doesn't. It depends on
who's doing it.
*105 Madison Avenue, New York, New York*

## Canadians Keep Zoloft in the Water Supply for Moments Like This

Customer service rep: Hey, when am I going to get my email
fixed? I have things that I need to send out to clients.
IT guy: Oh, yeah, we sent you an email requesting some
more information. We need you to send that email back
before we can fix your issue. . . . Hello? Are you sending
that email?
Customer service rep: [Hangs up.] I'm going on break now.
*1616 27th Avenue Northeast, Calgary, Alberta, Canada*

## No, It's "I Ripped Off My Nipples"

Employee #1: I waxed my chest last night, and I didn't have any more tape so I tried using duct tape.

Employee #2, laughing uncontrollably: Wait, wait, wait! I thought the punch line was, "I waxed my chest last night"!

*Lynchburg, Virginia*


## Situational Ethics

Coworker #1: Can you believe the whole company needs to take an ethics exam? It's online, but still . . .

Coworker #2: Yeah, it sucks. I heard that one department's doing the whole thing on a conference call together.

Coworker #1: But there's a test . . .

Coworker #2: Yeah, they're all taking the test together. One person says the answer and everybody enters it on their screen after the first person confirms it's right.

*Midtown, New York, New York*


## Who Among Us Can Say They Haven't Run That Search?

Employee #1: I don't think she got fired.

Employee #2: Yeah, but when they cleaned out her computer they found the search terms *Anal, Ann Coulter* quite frequently.

*18 Passaic Avenue, Fairfield, New Jersey*

coworkers

65

## Either That or a Pair of Pants

Maintenance tech #1: Animal Control is on the way to remove the dead skunk carcass. I'll let you know when they get here.

Maintenance tech #2: Uh, go ahead and call them back and tell them not to come. We checked it out and it's a used banana peel.

Maintenance tech #1: Ten-four.

*6400 Legacy Drive, Plano, Texas*

## Tell Me What You Think "Pornography" Is

Salesgirl: Wait, you know Pete*? Oh my god! You have to tell him that I miss jumping on the bed and making pornography with him. He'll know what I mean.

*L Street NW, Washington, DC*

## Oh, See, That One Was *Way* Too Detailed

Employee on phone: And how do you know her? And . . . how . . . do . . . you . . . know . . . her? . . . *And . . . how* . . . What do you mean, "Ask less detailed questions"?!

*Toronto, Ontario, Canada*

## I'll Bet the Fax Machine Will Be More Understanding

Speaker on fax machine: Listen, you freakin' idiot, this is the third time in five minutes you're tryin' to fax something to a phone number.

Employee in adjacent cubicle, two minutes later: Yeah, hi, this is the freakin' idiot . . . [Loud screech.] Shit, now I dialed their fax number.

*Georgesville Road, Columbus, Ohio*

## Tonight on SportsChat: Wankers Talk Wanking

Designer: Gosh, I just hate when you're watching a porn and they cut to the guy's face. It's always such an unfortunate time. I should write a letter of complaint.

IT guy: Yeah, if you only had a free hand.

*Leverington Avenue, Philadelphia, Pennsylvania*

## Uh-huh . . . And the Address? 1600 Pennsylvania Avenue . . . Got It.

Employee #1 on phone: Good morning, sir, my name is Brad,* and I'm from an execution service agency.

Employee #2: Dude. It's *executive search* agency!

*Den Bosch, Netherlands*

## During an Office Fire, Some Employees Will Run Directly into the Flames

Coworker #1: Where are we supposed to meet for the tornado drill?

Coworker #2: Beth* said that we can just stay at our desks, because we're already in the basement. She'll come around and do a head count.

Coworker #1: So we don't have to go outside, then?

Coworker #2: Um . . . no.

*7000 Portage Road, Kalamazoo, Michigan*


## Unveiling the Official Phallic Status Symbol for the Twenty-First Century

Customer service rep: Hey, your phone's open!

Courier: [Looks at his crotch.]

*1813 East 9th Street, Hopkinsville, Kentucky*


## By French Standards, He Got an Obsequiously Polite Person on the Phone

Employee on phone with French company: I'm sorry that you're offended that I don't speak French, sir. . . . Well, I don't know what to tell you. I speak English and Korean, I just don't speak French. We have a great offer here. I think you'd like to hear about it, even in English. . . . Well, if you'd like I can speak to you with what French I *do* know, but I'm afraid it will only be "hello" and "yes" or "no." . . . I'm sorry that you think my lack of French represents what's wrong with America in general. . . .

*61 Broadway, New York, New York*

## And Leaving Early from Happy Hour to Shoot Heroin into My Eyelids

Cube rat #1: I quit smoking last week.
Cube rat #2: How's that going?
Cube rat #1: Well, I'm leaving early to go drinking.

*St. Louis, Missouri*

## Dressing in Hefty Bags Gives You a Certain Latitude

Female cube dweller: Good news! Remember that smell I kept smelling but couldn't find? That garbage smell? It was me!

*1009 Lenox Drive, Lawrenceville, New Jersey*

## No, but I Can Claim Sexual Harassment for Your Use of the Phrase "Rock-Hard Nipples"

Creative director: It's so cold in here, my rock-hard nipples are chafing on my shirt. Can I claim workers' comp for that?

*Radio station, Ottawa, Ontario, Canada*

## Who's One Beer Short of a Six-Pack?

Bartender #1: How many beers are in a six-pack?
Bartender #2: I work with a fucking idiot.

*Subiaco, Australia*

## But I'm the Janitor!

Account biller #1: Let me ask you something—what am I supposed to do with those claims the boss just gave me?
Account biller #2: Your job, perhaps?

*Memphis, Tennessee*

## That's the Special Benefit

Coworker reading email: Can you believe this shit?! The nerve! "For those over fifty, special healthcare benefits." Over fifty! How can they send me this shit and . . . Oh, there's a free lunch . . . Well, maybe I'll go.

*Trinity Place, New York, New York*

## Why Generation Y Already Outearns Generation X

Assistant: You ever do something repeatedly—so much that you're like, "Whoa, this isn't real. I'm not doing this"?
Intern: Ummm . . .
Assistant: Like, when you're staring at your face in the mirror for so long that you're like, "Whoa! That's not my

face! This isn't real!" Hasn't that ever happened to you?

Intern: No. That's usually when I stop drinking.

*900 2nd Street NE, Washington, DC*


## Don't Hate the Player, Hate the Desk

Girl grunt: Can you keep this desk clean?

Guy grunt: What? The desk is clean. Stop hating!

Girl grunt: Hey, hey, don't say that, I'm not a cock-blocker. I don't cock-block.

Guy grunt: What the fuck does that have to do with my desk?

*350 South Figueroa, Los Angeles, California*


## Then I Got to Thinking That Maybe I *Am* Julie and Don't Know It

Coworker: Hello?

Voice on phone: Is Julie there?

Coworker: No, I'm sorry, but you have the wrong number.

Voice on phone: Oh, okay, sorry.

Coworker: No problem. [Phone immediately rings again.] Listen, man, you have the wrong number.

Voice on phone: Are you sure this is your number? I checked, and this is the same number that my friend Julie gave me. Could you call your number and ask her to call me back?

Coworker: Sure, just as soon as I get off the phone with you. [Hangs up phone.] Jackass.

*1200 Sovereign Row, Oklahoma City, Oklahoma*

## I Repose That You're Right

Girl: So I told them to just go ahead and ship the extra reports to our suppository in—

Guy: Wait, I'm sorry, what did you just say? Did you say, "ship the reports to the suppository"?

Girl: Yeah . . .

Guy: Um, it's "repository." *Sup*positories are pills that go in your ass. . . .

Girl: Fuck.

*Route 1 South, Princeton, New Jersey*


## It's What She Would Want If She Weren't Selfishly Preoccupied with Her Little Personal Problems

Coworker #1: And who ordered the salad?

Coworker #2: Marie,* but she left for the day.

Coworker #1: Is she okay?

Coworker #2: I hope so. She was crying when she left. I guess the police called and said her seven-year-old daughter was a town over from where she was supposed to be, and no one knows where the sitter went.

Coworker #1: Oh, that's awful. [Long pause.] So, you think that means I can eat her salad?

*Providence, Rhode Island*


## No, I Quit Because None of Them Were Prostitutes

Male admin: So, are you a prostitute?

Female admin: Excuse me?

Male admin: It's a line from that movie *Monster*.

Female admin: You can't just go around saying things like that to people.

Male admin: Oh. Well, I used to do it all the time at my old job.

Female admin: Is that why you're not working there anymore?

*Connecticut Avenue, Washington, DC*

## Except Today They Were Spouting Some Nonsense about Loving My Neighbor

Coworker #1: What radio station do you listen to on your way to work?

Coworker #2: I listen to a Christian station so I can prepare myself for dealing with you assholes.

*Dallas, Texas*

## You Should Hear Her Go Off on People Who Say, "Between You and I"

Employee #1: Jane* says that she feels nauseous. I think she's going home.

Employee #2: Well, Jane should take a course in English vocabulary, because if she feels nausea, then she feels "nauseated," not "nauseous." To be nauseous is to be disgusting or foul.

Employee #1: You're kinda a bitch.

*Hadley Road, South Plainfield, New Jersey*

## Which Was Named after the McDonald's Clown and That Suicide Girl

Employee #1: So, how do we go about naming our aircraft?

Employee #2: Well, the reserve has a plane named *The Spirit of Ronald Reagan*.

Employee #1: Who is that named after?

Boss: It's named after the airport, I think.

*Pentagon, Arlington, Virginia*

## No, That Kind Really Sucks

Twenty-ish lunch breaker #1: Yeah, can I get a ham and cheese sandwich on fellatio bread?

Twenty-ish lunch breaker #2: Ummm, I think it's called "focaccia" bread. . . .

*Lafayette, Indiana*

## What You Just Snorted Two Of?

Reading tutor #1: It's your turn.

Reading tutor #2: Shut up, I know. I'm thinking. [Places letter on Scrabble board.] There.

Reading tutor #3: What's a gee-ram?

Reading tutor #2: "Gram," you idiot.

*Elementary school, New Orleans, Louisiana*

## And I Expect to Be Hung Over Monday

Suit #1: I'm going to need that project done for Monday. Can you get on that right now?

Suit #2: It's Friday, and I have beer to drink. It's really going to have to wait.

*4881 Yonge Street, Toronto, Ontario, Canada*


## That's My Kind of Morning Update!

Staffer #1: Well, thanks, everyone, for not telling me my fly was open.

Staffer #2: Your fly was open?

Staffer #1: Yes. I just now looked down, and there it was, wide open! You didn't notice?

Staffer #2: Well, I don't spend a large portion of the day staring at your crotch.

Staffer #3: Yeah, I only do it during our morning update meetings.

*10 Medical Center Boulevard, Winston-Salem, North Carolina*


## The Real Reason Behind the Great Chicago Fire

Engineer #1: If you *flush the toilet*, you lose water pressure?! So, it's like, "Sorry, the dishwasher is running. We have no fire protection."

Engineer #2: Who flushes the toilet if their house is on fire?

*700 West Capitol Avenue, Little Rock, Arkansas*

## Tragically, This Misinformation Prevented Debbie from Having Her Bullet Wound Treated

Employee #1: I went to the bathroom, and I have a big hole right in the middle of my crotch.

Employee #2: We all do, sweetie. It's called a vagina.

*1907 West Sycamore Street, Kokomo, Indiana*

## In Fairness, He Was Cross-Dressing at the Time

Construction worker #1: So, you know how I knew you were gay?

Construction worker #2: *What?*

Construction worker #1: It's cool, dude. But know how I knew?

Construction worker #2: [Shakes head.]

Construction worker #1: When you started making out with me at happy hour last week.

Construction worker #2: Oh. Oh, yeah.

*1670 Broadway, Denver, Colorado*

## I Tried Putting a Floppy in Her Once . . . Nothing

Computer guy #1: I can't see the hard drive on this network.

Computer guy #2: Well, the problem is that the disk isn't mounted. First you have to mount Claire.*

Claire: Hey!

Computer guy #2: "Claire" is the name of the office hard drive.

*701 South Mount Vernon Avenue, San Bernardino, California*

## Why Nigerian Emails Work

Coworker viewing a MySpace page: Jeff Buckley's online!
He's dead, how is he doing this?!

*Frances Avenue, Lancaster, Pennsylvania*


## Well, It's a Huge Job to Turn the Glass Around

Five maintenance engineers stand staring at a window with
rain pouring down on the inside of the glass.
Engineer: If we all knew about this, why didn't we fix it?

*6th & Sycamore Streets, Cincinnati, Ohio*


## Is That Better or Worse Than Her Stepdaughter Being Pregnant and Moving Out to Live with the Son?

Coworker #1: Well, I got some good news and some bad
news last night.
Coworker #2: Let me guess . . . Your stepdaughter's moving out, but she's pregnant.
Coworker #1: Oh my god, you're so close! My stepdaughter's moving out and my eighteen-year-old son's girlfriend is pregnant.
Coworker #2: Wow, what luck.

*1649 Pandosy Street, Kelowna, British Columbia, Canada*

coworkers

## The Scary Thing Is, I Agree with Both of Them

Male coworker: It just ticks me off that Elmo is more popular than Grover. My other job was really boring, and one day I was fantasizing—
Female coworker: I think we've heard enough.

*20890 Kenbridge Court, Lakeville, Minnesota*

## She Waits on Her Roof for Aliens Every Night

Female cashier: Hey, is that your purple car out there?
Stock dude: Yeah, it is. The chicks love it.
Female cashier: I like it. I want a purple Probe.
Stock dude: Yeah, I heard that about you.

*436 Southbridge Street, Auburn, Massachusetts*

## Why Don't You Give It to Me Now So I Can Call You Later and Get It from You?

Suit #1: Why didn't you call me?
Suit #2: I didn't have your number.
Suit #1: If you called me I could have given it to you.

*32nd Street, Jersey City, New Jersey*

## So If You're So Smart, How Do They Put Out the Fires, Then?

Man #1: No, you're not fucking listening here. There are *no* fire hydrants in the *ocean*.
Man #2: But we could—

Man #1: Oh my god. No fire hydrants! Are you hearing me? *There are no fire hydrants in the ocean!*

*Insurance office, Woodbury, New York*

## Antie Maim

Employee #1: I noticed there were a few just walking around by themselves on my desk.

Employee #2: Those are scouts! Kill them or they'll go back and tell the others the coast is clear. Then you'll have a rope of them!

Employee #1: I know, so I tried breaking the legs on one of them hoping he'd go back and tell the others not to come, it's not safe, but all he did was walk around in circles on my desk, so I just smashed him.

*Atlanta, Georgia*

## She Stole a Kid from a Gay Couple? That Is Low.

Intern: Candace's* mom is sixty-five! And she's had seven kids from, like, eight different guys!

*1325 East-West Highway, Silver Spring, Maryland*

## Corporate Suicide Bombers

Employee: No one saw who took my chair? I hope I have crabs.

*345 Broadway, New York, New York*

## Could Have Happened to Any of Us

Office girl #1: What's wrong?

Office girl #2, gagging: I was miming committing suicide by glue stick, and I accidentally inhaled.

*North Michigan Avenue, Chicago, Illinois*

## Too Bad It's Another Part That Got the Clap

Girl worker #1: My boyfriend is in the pen.

Girl worker #2: For how long?

Girl worker #1: He's been there for three years.

Girl worker #2: Wow! You've been faithful to him for three years?

Girl worker #1: My heart has been. . . .

*2720 Villa Promenade, Oklahoma City, Oklahoma*

## Turn Racism into a Fun Office Game!

Coworker #1: I would have been up all night with my shotgun.

Coworker #2: Why? The cops already had the perpetrator.

Coworker #1: Whatever, you're just saying that because he was black. . . . Otherwise he would have just been a *suspect*.

Coworker #2: Ummm, the guy was white. I never said he was black. All I said was he wasn't wearing shoes.

*Pacific Drive, Lexington Park, Maryland*

## It Cleans Those Leather-Belt Wounds Right Up

Loan officer: My husband's parents were married for fifty
    years.
Receptionist: What's the secret of being married that long?
Collector: Alcohol.

*802 South Westnedge Avenue, Kalamazoo, Michigan*


## Colorado: It's Out of This World (Allegedly)

Worker #1: Oh, didn't I tell you I'm moving to Colorado?
Worker #2: Really? When?
Worker #1: I leave next week, but I decided I would move to
    Colorado when I was six. That's when I heard John Den-
    ver sing "Rocky Mountain High."
Worker #2: That's why you're moving to Colorado?
Worker #1: Well, and because it's so hot here because of all
    the global warming going on. You know, they don't have
    that in Colorado.

*Fairfield County, Connecticut*


## What If Your Kid's Hung Over?

Coworker #1: Kids are just a built-in excuse to call in sick. If
    Carl* can call in because his kid is sick, I should be able
    to call in sick because I'm hung over.
Coworker #2: Wouldn't that be every day, then?
Coworker #1: No, I mean too hung over to work.

*Highways 7 & 78, Independence, Missouri*

## 2006: Al Qaeda Reaches Alaska

Admin: Do you need help with anything?
Engineer: Nobody ever asks that here. What are you up to?

*Anchorage, Alaska*

## Actually, She Details Cars Professionally

Account manager: So, I sent you that new job applicant. Have fun.

Recruiter: I just opened it up. Wow, she completely misspelled "Delaware" state.

Account manager: Oh, it gets worse.

Recruiter: "Seven years" with an exclamation point . . . And she spelled "with" wrong!

Account manager: Yep, and she's a "detail-oriented professional."

*Trolley Square, Wilmington, Delaware*

## Solitaire Is a Conspiracy by the Black Man to Undermine White Productivity

Employee #1: Blacks, blacks everywhere! Stupid blacks! I can't do anything with them. They just take over.

Employee #2: Cletus,* quit playing solitaire and do some work.

*Missoula, Montana*

## Should I Wait to Be Invited to the Celebration or Just Invite Myself?

Male employee to female employee: Now, hold on. You just
   wait until I whip it right out. . . . Then we can celebrate.
Nearby male coworker: I feel so uncomfortable right now.

*Louisville, Kentucky*


## Thank God I Have This NyQuil in My Desk

Worker #1: I went to all the liquor stores this morning, and
   they were closed. They don't open until 10 a.m.
Worker #2: Well, that's retarded. Haven't they ever heard of
   mimosas?
Worker #1: Or alcoholics?

*37 West 20th Street, New York, New York*


## What the Fire Said

Guy over PA system: May I have your attention, please?
   There has been a fire reported in the building.
Coworker: Well, that's just an excuse to go smoke.

*East 13th Street, Cleveland, Ohio*


## Oh, Shoot, It's Time to Go

Office peon #1: When do you leave for the trip?
Office peon #2: In about twenty minutes.
Office peon #1: Well, are you jizzed?
Office peon #2: What?

Office peon #1: Jizzed. You know, excited!

Office peon #2: Uh, sure.

*Red Run Boulevard, Owings Mills, Maryland*


## They Should Get Married

Giddy coworker: You like alcohol, don't you?

Stoic coworker: I like when everyone around me is drunk. It makes my life easier.

Giddy coworker: I like when I'm drunk. It makes my life easier.

*10 Exchange Place, Jersey City, New Jersey*


## Why I Started Eating Lunch in My Car

Employee #1: What the fuck?! This sandwich is impossible.

Employee #2: It looks like a big, gaping vagina.

Employee #1: It's like eating out a big vagina. Look! Chunks are falling off!

Employee #2: Your sandwich has an STD! Like hooker poon.

Employee #3, holding identical sandwich missing a single bite: Well, looks like I'm done. If anyone wants my dirty vagina sandwich, you're welcome to it. Thanks for the lunch convo.

*Worcester, Massachusetts*


## I Said, "Him Pet Us." American Is Good Doggy

European grunt: Did you just use the word *impetus*? I think you're the first American I have heard use that word.

*3695 Freedom Circle, Santa Clara, California*

## The Concept of Caring Was Not Covered at MIT— Please Explain

Engineer #1: So, how's it going?

Engineer #2: Crazy. Completely crazy. Why do you ask?

Engineer #1: Because I care, dumbass.

*500 Howard Street, San Francisco, California*


## Worried It Might Get Chicago Wet

Coworker #1: Did it rain while you were in Chicago?

Coworker #2: Nope.

Coworker #1: Oh, that's good. I saw on the Weather Channel that it was raining in Virginia, and I got worried.

*42 South Street, Hopkinton, Massachusetts*


## Would You Like to *Sue* Maury? Because We Can Help You There.

Receptionist on phone: Hello, law offices . . . Excuse me? I think you have the wrong number. This is a law office. . . . No, this law office has nothing to do with the *Maury Show*. Sir, you know, I really think you have the wrong number. . . . No, our number is nothing like that. . . . Well, I don't know, are you drunk? Really? Well, good for you. . . . Okay, well, good luck in getting through to Maury.

*350 5th Avenue, New York, New York*

## It's Really More About Where They Land, Isn't It?

Peon: I wanted to show you this order. I think someone dropped the ball.

Sales associate: Let's see whose order it is. . . . Oh, it's Ryan's,* and he's out this week.

Peon: Uh-oh.

Sales associate: See what happens when you go on vacation? Your balls get dropped!

*8220 England Street, Charlotte, North Carolina*

## Why Rich Babies Get Fetal Alcohol Syndrome

Worker bee #1: I'm very tired. I went out last night.

Worker bee #2: Oh, did you have a lot to drink?

Worker bee #1: Of course not, I'm pregnant.

Worker bee #2: It's pretty bad to drink when you're pregnant.

Worker bee #1: Yeah, it's so expensive, and you've gotta save money to buy baby stuff.

*Goulbourn Street, Sydney, Australia*

## She's Jockeying for "Most Improved"

Employee #1: Where's Anne*?

Employee #2: I dunno, but she's sure going to be late to her time management training class.

*980 Kelly Johnson Drive, Las Vegas, Nevada*

## Probably Far Enough

Male worker: I put on the tutu, and that was as far as I got.

*4900 Tiedemann Road, Brooklyn, Ohio*


## I Know the Perfect Position for You!

Employee #1: I don't know how you got a better review than you did last year.

Employee #2: Yeah, me either.

Employee #1: You know, I really only get about 50 percent out of you each day.

Employee #2: Yeah, that sounds about right. Some days more, some days less . . . Usually less.

Employee #1: Wouldn't it be great if I got that 100 percent out of you, though?

Employee #2: Probably, but I really just don't feel like it.

*901 Warrenville Road, Chicago, Illinois*


## No, I Have a Plane Ticket and a Shovel

Lady peon #1: I'm saving myself for Mozart.

Lady peon #2: That's going to be quite a wait, honey.

*Santa Fe, New Mexico*


## And Just Like That, the Headache Was Gone

Coworker #1: Will you come over and put a cold compress on my head?

coworkers

Coworker #2: Sure, what do you want me to wear?

*355 Park Avenue, New York, New York*

## Being a Muppet Is Not a Choice—They're Made That Way

Security guard #1: You hear about that wedding today? Someone's gettin' married in the park.
Security guard #2: Who? Bert and Ernie?
Security guard #3: Not in this state.

*Langhorne, Pennsylvania*

## When You've Had That Many 'Shrooms, Who Can Be Sure?

Dude burger flipper: What did you do this weekend?
Chick burger flipper: I went to Ohio for a concert.
Dude burger flipper: Ohio? You went all the way over by California for a concert?
Chick burger flipper: Ummm . . . No . . .

*Fast-food restaurant, Rhode Island*

## Oh, Sorry: The Thingamajig Was Fubarred by the Whatzit and Corrupted Your Jimmyjam

Tech guy: Yeah, so I tried to open the file, and it said, "Something, something, file can't open, something."
Client services girl: Gee, thanks, Tech!

*1619 Broadway, New York, New York*

## One EggBeater Experience Is Enough

Employee #1: Okay, I'm taking breakfast orders for the meeting. What do you guys want?

Employee #2: Ummm, I'll have the Western omelet.

Employee #1: Okay.

Employee #2: Oh, wait . . . Are there eggs in that?

Employee #1: Uh, yeah!

Employee #2: Okay then!

*Falls Church, Virginia*


## Better Hope English Doesn't Become the Official Language of the U.S.

Fool: He said he had a stomachache so I gave him some Aflac—you know, Rolodex?

Coworker: Antacids? Rolaids?

*7th Street & Congress Avenue, Austin, Texas*


## The Ends Justify the Means

Builder #1: Do we have a hole puncher?

Builder #2: Yeah, it's over there near Diane's* fat arse.

Builder #1: You can't say that! That's sexual harassment! Diane, don't worry, love. You've got a great arse.

*Construction site office, Townsville, Australia*

## Plus, They Poop All over Your Suit

Male coworker: I don't understand why taking your baby on your lap in an airplane is such a bad idea.

Female coworker: Dude, what if you crash? That can't be safe.

Male coworker: You're right, I guess. Babies probably don't make great flotation devices.

*590 North Shore Drive, Milwaukee, Wisconsin*


## My Floors Are Wax-Only

Coworker #1: What's a carpet-muncher? Is that a new slang for "vacuum cleaner"?

Coworker #2: Um, no. Hehehe . . . I'll give you a thousand bucks if you ask the boss for a carpet-muncher.

Coworker #1: Why? I don't have carpeting.

*800 East 28th Street, Minneapolis, Minnesota*


## If He's an Idiot and Can Steal Your Clients, That Makes You What?

Sales guy: Jason,* quit calling into my sales territory! You are a freaking poacher!

Jason: Poacher? I don't even like eggs.

Sales guy: You're an idiot.

*6400 Congress Avenue, Boca Raton, Florida*

## It's Either That or Get One of Those Helper Monkeys

Editor #1: I have finger toes.

Photographer: You mean, like, long and bony?

Editor #1: Yeah. I can, like, pick stuff up with them.

Editor #2: Do you pinch people with them?

Editor #1: Yeah, I always pinch [my wife]. She hates it.

Editor #2: God is just preparing you for when you lose your arms.

*333 North Meridian, Oklahoma City, Oklahoma*


## Guy's a Total Psycho. I Broke Up with Him Months Ago, but He Won't Stop Calling.

Intern answering phone: Good afternoon, Science Committee. . . . Mike,* Buzz Aldrin is on the line.

Mike, rolling his eyes: Oh, shit.

*Rayburn House Building, Washington, DC*


## This Is Making Me Hungry

Office grunt #1: Who was chief then?

Office grunt #2: According to the record, Dick Chase.*

Office grunt #3: Wait, Dick Chase? So, if he were filling out a form today, last name first, he'd be . . .

Office grunt #1: You're right! Case closed, that says it all!

*26 Federal Plaza, New York, New York*

## But You Will Need to Bring in a Wire So I Can Hang Myself Later

Desk clerk on phone: No, ma'am, you don't need a cable for
the wireless network.

*328 West Lane Avenue, Columbus, Ohio*


## But It's That Kind of Go-Get-'Em Attitude That Makes It So Hard for Me to Retire

Coworker #1: So, your last day is coming up, right?

Coworker #2: Yeah, thank God for that.

Coworker #1: I wonder who they will replace you with.
Maybe the homeless guy on the street. . . . I bet he could
do as good as you.

Coworker #2: I'm not sure I like your style.

*Santa Monica, California*


## I Still Prefer It to "Fuck You!"

Off-duty employee: Don't you just hate when you're working and you say, "Have a nice day," and you don't mean
it, and the person knows you don't mean it but you have
to say it anyway?

Cashier: Yeah, totally. [To customer] Thanks! Have a nice
day!

*Harrisonburg, Virginia*

## It's My Fitness Program

Female coworker: Yeah, these bruises on my legs? I wish I could say they were from S and M. Actually, I was just drunkenly stumbling around.

*33 New Montgomery Street, San Francisco, California*


## Sarah Tobias: Too Late

Female employee: Man, I'm sooo busy today. Why is everyone taking advantage of me?
Male employee: I don't know.
Female employee: Oh, well, maybe I just let people take advantage of me. It's just easier that way.
Male employee: Some advice: don't ever say that in a *bar*.

*1301 East Algonquin Road, Chicago, Illinois*


## She Got Pregnant During a Gang Bang

Coworker #1: My sister just had her baby this morning!
Coworker #2: How exciting! Wait, who just had a baby last month?
Coworker #1: My sister.
Coworker #2: The same one?

*1700 Montgomery Street, San Francisco, California*

## Could We Talk About Baltimore Again, Please?

White coworker: So, you're from Baltimore, right?

Black coworker: No, everyone thinks all there is to Maryland is Baltimore. I'm actually from a small town called Upper Marlboro, which is closer to D.C.

White coworker: Really? Baltimore is cool. Is where you're from like Baltimore?

Black coworker: Oh, no, it's very different. In fact, people from Baltimore don't like people from PG [County] so much. They say we're bourgeois, stuck up, and that we act like white people. But we don't act white, we just have money.

*29th Street, New York, New York*

## Oh, Who Am I Kidding? We Are *Absolutely* Going Back There.

Coworker: Well, then we've got something to do next week. But we're not going back to that place. It was nasty. My van smells like a hooker died in it.

*111 Oak Street, Bonner Springs, Kansas*

## It's Important for Friends to Do Things Together, Don't You Think?

Receptionist on phone: So, I was throwing up in the bathroom, and my three best friends were having sex in the stall next to me.

*1601 Cloverfield Boulevard, Santa Monica, California*

## Geez, You Don't Leave Me Much Room to Maneuver

Coworker #1: Hey, I got a new joke. Anyone want to hear it?
Coworker #2: Not if it involves poop.
Coworker #3: Or chickens.

*Washington, DC*

## What If Your Coworker's an Asshole?

Assistant #1: What if you get a busy signal?
Assistant #2: That means it's busy.
Assistant #1, after long pause: Thank you.

*450 North Street, Sacramento, California*

## Next Time Break Up Via Email

Employee on phone: You are a psycho if you think you'll break up with me over the phone! What am I supposed to say to a psycho? What am I supposed to say to a psycho? What am I supposed to say to a psycho?!
Coworker: For my sake you can say good-bye to a psycho!

*5760 Highway 80, Pearl, Mississippi*

## Might Have Swallowed the Spring, the Way the Conversation's Bouncing Around

Coworker #1: Well, one time I was eating here, and I found a piece of metal in my mouth! You know, a long thin piece, but bunched up. I chewed on it and it, like, exploded in my mouth. In my mouth! Can you believe it? It was all twisted or something. Coiled. Oh, yeah. It was a spring! A spring! Anyway, I chewed on it and it, like, boinged in my mouth. Wait, wait, wait. Can you believe it? Boing, boing, boing! So I spit it out and look at it and think, "What the hell is this and what is it doing in my food?" But really, can you believe it? Boinging all over the place!

Coworker #2: Okay. Enough already. You're making me sick. It's like having lunch with Roseanne Roseannadanna. Next you'll be telling me about the time you found a toe-nail in your cheeseburger.

Coworker #1: Oh, yeah. Wouldn't that be great? Lunch with Roseanne. But she's dead, you know. Cancer.

Coworker #2: Gilda Radner died of cancer.

Coworker #1: Who? Why are you always changing the subject?

Coworker #2: I'm eating at my desk.

*Hospital and clinics cafeteria, 1500 University Avenue, Madison, Wisconsin*

## Or Something

Employee #1: Where is Great Britain?

Employee #2: I think it's a city in Scotland or something.

*Toronto, Ontario, Canada*

## And What about Grave Robbers? Sometimes They'll Kill You Just to Get Your Jewelry.

Lady coworker #1: It's so scary hearing about people dying.
Lady coworker #2: Yeah, totally . . . You can die from so many things. You can die from death, sickness . . .

*Sydney, Australia*

## He Doesn't Recognize Countries That Achieved Independence after 1800

Male employee #1: How did Costa Rica go in the World Cup?
Male employee #2: Who does he play for?
Male employee #1: Are you serious?
Male employee #2: What? Is he on the Australian team or something? Is that why I'm meant to know him?

*Perth, Australia*

## And What's a "Document"?

Employee: Hey, Bertha,* can you help me send a fax? It's been so long since I've had to use this.
Bertha: Okay, well, put your document faceup here, and then enter the number here, and press Start.
Employee: What number?
Bertha: The fax number you're sending to . . .
Employee: Oh, am I supposed to know that?

*208 Raleigh Street, Chapel Hill, North Carolina*

coworkers

## Why Can't You Be Like Mulan? She Was Asian, but She Could Take a Punch!

Asian coworker to black coworker: Why can't you be like Akeelah in *Akeelah and the Bee*? She was black, but she could spell!

*235 East 42nd Street, New York, New York*


## EEOC's Favorite Kind of Testimony

Employee: Oh, someone took a picture of the cock again! Only it doesn't have sunglasses anymore.

*101 Hillpointe Drive, Canonsburg, Pennsylvania*


## No, the Birth Took Place over a Span of Four Years

Admin #1: How old is his son?

Admin #2: Ten.

Admin #1: And how many kids does he have?

Admin #2: Three. They're triplets.

Admin #1: And they're all ten?

*Route 1 South, Princeton, New Jersey*


## Actually, That's What Happened to My Ankles

Sales guy: How can you sit like that? It's disgusting.

Information specialist: I have weak ankles. I'm sorry I disgust you.

Sales guy: You don't disgust me, just the way you sit. Besides, you're always making fun of my women.

Information specialist: Say, do you have one of those auto-lifts in your bedroom?

Sales guy: I see what you're saying. Because I like big women . . .

Information specialist: I mean, in case you get pinned or something.

Sales guy: Funny thing is I know how to maneuver one of those, from a previous job.

Information specialist: I'll take that as a yes.

*Washington, DC*


## This Memo's Gonna Get Me That Promotion

Coworker #1: *Ew!*

Coworker #2: What?

Coworker #1: His Internet history has porn on it!

Coworker #2: Really?

Coworker #1: Yeah!

Coworker #2: Like what?

Coworker #1: A whole bunch of free stuff from [Porno*] dot com. I can't believe this!

Coworker #2: Yeah, I know . . .

Coworker #1: I mean . . . I don't care if he does this at home, but not at this computer . . . We work in here!

Coworker #2: Yeah . . . Sure . . . What was that site again?

*41 West Clinton Avenue, Tenafly, New Jersey*

## People Talk about Chipmunks Only on Planets without Atmospheres

Peon #1: Weather is the great conversational equalizer.
Peon #2: Yeah.
Peon #1: 'Cause every place has weather. And chipmunks. But nobody ever talks about chipmunks.

*1593 Galbraith Avenue, Grand Rapids, Michigan*

## They Say, "Come Talk to Us When the Dead Answer You"

New Age employee: Yeah, my granddaughter is an Indigo child—she can talk to the dead. But, if you ask me, her parents really aren't doing enough with her talent.

*1712 Spring Garden Street, Greensboro, North Carolina*

## At the Urban Legend Semifinals

Assistant #1: Did you know that one of the ingredients in gum is coyote urine?
Assistant #2: Did you know that there's something in cat urine that causes schizophrenia?

*Buckhead Loop, Atlanta, Georgia*

## You Also Gotta Refrain from Calling It "The Gerbil"

Sales guy #1: You're nasty!
Sales guy #2: I'm not the one that took the pictures on that site.

Sales guy #1: I'm not the one that's talking about shaving my gerbil!

Sales guy #2: Oooh . . . You gotta shave the gerbil. You *gotta*!

*8220 England Street, Charlotte, North Carolina*


## Dear Diary, If I Can Just Drink Less at Lunch, She Will Be Mine

Contracts officer: Frankly, I think she'll be tickled shitless. . . . I could have said she'd be shittled titless, but I thought that would be offensive.

HR lady: This meeting has now officially gone on too long.

*1010 North Glebe Road, Arlington, Virginia*


## She Knows Where Jimmy Hoffa Is, Though

Desk assistant: So, what happens if we go on strike? Do we not come to work?

*CBS Broadcast Center, 524 West 57th Street, New York, New York*


## . . . Mom

Coworker on phone: Uh, yes, this is Aaron Jones* with the Benson Mortgage Company.* It's Wednesday, 10:30 a.m.—I'm sorry! It's just that, well, you sounded like a voicemail voice.

*1350 Deming Way, Middleton, Wisconsin*

## I'm *So* Almost over Her

Office drone #1: Last week I was on MySpace, and I dropped my old high school girlfriend a line. Would you see this as being friendly or creepy?

Office drone #2: Well, did you search specifically for her?

Office drone #1: No, I seriously just happened across her through my high school's page, but unbeknownst to me she had just recently set up her account. I'm just freaked out that it looks like I've been trolling the Internet waters waiting for her to surface and then, *bam!* Ten years ago that would have been the case, but not now.

*Liberty Drive, Bloomington, Indiana*

## She Was *Breast-Feeding*, You Sicko

Coworker on phone: . . . And I like them already—they seem pretty cool. Nothing like starting my day with a cute chick showing me her boob. . . .

*Alpharetta, Georgia*

## He's Got a Lot of Pull, Though

Coworker: Oh, you know how he is. . . . Yeah, that's a great word to describe him—*Wanker.*

*Madison, Connecticut*

## That Depends on How Nice Your Car Is

Worker bee: Let's go for a ride. Does your top come off?

*150 Batson Drive, Manchester, Connecticut*


## Teens Really Should Be Cleaning *That* Up Themselves

Coworker #1: So, my Ob-Gyn has been seeing all these young girls for their annuals this summer. She was amazed at how much sex they're having—like, two to three times a day. She had to tell them they had to stop having intercourse for a month so the pill could take effect, and they say, "What are we supposed to do all summer?" She was shocked.

Coworker #2: How old are these girls?

Coworker #1: She said they're between seventeen and twenty years old.

Coworker #2: Geez. Even if I had time to have sex two times a day I'd have better things to do!

Coworker #1: Yeah, like clean up after my teenagers!

*Motor vehicle building, Trenton, New Jersey*


## At Last, an RDA Is Established for Cookies

Drone #1: I am trying really hard to stay away from these cookies on my desk.

Drone #2: Oh my god, tell me about it. Those cookies are *good*.

coworkers

Drone #1: Maybe if I look at how many calories they have, it'll be easier to stay away. One cookie, a hundred and twenty calories.

Drone #3: Well, how many calories are you supposed to have?

Drone #1: I don't know. I think two thousand calories is supposed to be average.

Drone #3: And the cookies are a hundred and twenty? Then you can eat all you want!

*8220 England Street, Charlotte, North Carolina*


## I Hear They Have a Rivalry with the Fallujah Branch

Coworker #1: What branch of the military was he in?

Coworker #2: In the USA branch.

*Madison, Wisconsin*


## Memo to All Staff: There Will Be a Meeting to Discuss What Can Be Done to Curtail the Number of Meetings

Office grunt #1: I hate all these fucking meetings!

Office grunt #2: Didn't you set this meeting up?

Office grunt #1: Yeah, but that's not the point.

*Oil company office, Houston, Texas*

## Fuck You, You Felch-Sucking, Mung-Eating, Necrotic, Limp-Dicked Father-Raper

Drone #1: Crikey Moses! Who the hell wants their picture taken in the Mastermind chair?

Drone #2: "Crikey Moses"?! You need some better swear words!

*201 Wood Lane, London, England*


## He's an Art Teacher

Coworker: I sent out the class rosters for summer term to all the faculty and got an email back from one guy wanting to know why he can't find his name on the list. . . . Because it's the list of his *students*! How did he get to be a teacher?!

*1400 Penn Avenue, Pittsburgh, Pennsylvania*


## Get the Mirror off Your Desk

Employee: I've been on email since 5 a.m., and all I see is incomptitude.

*550 South Hope Street, Los Angeles, California*


## "So Peaceful You Could Cut It with a Knife," I Said

Circulation clerk: I was talking to her about how peaceful it is in here, and now she's going to go get a knife.

*1035 North Treat Avenue, Tucson, Arizona*

### "Steaming the Laundry," from Page 949 of the *Kama Sutra*

Coworker: You need to preheat your hoo-ha. This is too much.
Intern: We're still talking about the steaming the laundry, right?

*Theater, Brunswick, Maine*


### Hey, I've Got Some Straw in the Corner of My Office. Want to Watch It Turn into Worms?

Coworker #1: Do you have to dust your desk all the time with your window shade open?
Coworker #2: No, why?
Coworker #1: Because of all the sun.
Coworker #2: Huh?
Coworker #1: Dust comes from sunlight.

*4725 North Scottsdale Road, Scottsdale, Arizona*


### Is He Related to That Blond Kid Who Plays Guitar on the Disney Channel?

Tech guy #1: Jimmy Carter's son has a MySpace page.
Tech guy #2: Who the hell is Jimmy Carter?

*600 Pennsylvania Avenue, Washington, DC*


### I Can Sell Her Anything!

Assistant on phone: Let me see if she's available. . . .
Ellen,* do you want to talk to a Janie* at U.S., Inc.*?

Ellen: She's a dumbass . . . Yeah, I want to talk to her.

*8220 England Street, Charlotte, North Carolina*

## Right Next to Malibu Eva Braun

Human resources employee: That's not GI Joe, that's *Hitler*!

*National Geographic Offices, Washington, DC*

## If a New Jersey Resident Falls in His Kitchen and No One Is Around to See It, Is It Still Funny?

Drone #1: Well, you should move to New Jersey. There are great apartments in my complex.

Drone #2: I don't know that I want to move out there.

Drone #1: The apartments are great—lots of closet space, granite countertops in the kitchen . . .

Drone #2: I don't want granite counters. If I fell and hit my head on them it would hurt.

*1 Liberty Plaza, New York, New York*

## Two Weeks, Even

Girl #1: It doesn't really feel like Friday.

Girl #2: What does it feel like?

Girl #1: I don't know . . . It feels like a week from Friday.

*220 Kroncke Drive, Sun Prairie, Wisconsin*

## We're Flying One in from St. Petersburg

Female employee on phone: . . . Will you outsource the foreskin?

*18th Street & Park Avenue, New York, New York*

## Viagra?

Customer service rep waving papers around: How do you get the thingy to do the stuff?

*323 East Grand River, Howell, Michigan*

## Yeah, I Think the Nigerians Took That Over in the Fifties

Coworker #1: So, is Mumbai, like, a country that we do business with?

Coworker #2: No, it's a city! It used to be called Bombay before those imperialist American jerks finally pulled out and the native people got their land back.

Coworker #1: Oh . . . So it was Moscow that was the country I was thinking of?

Coworker #2: Probably.

*41st Avenue, Calgary, Alberta, Canada*

## Or Whatever It's Called When You Drink Too Much and Fall Asleep

Peon: I swear, I keep falling asleep at my desk. . . . I think I have epilepsy.

*7945 Haven Avenue, Rancho Cucamonga, California*

## It Took a Lawsuit for the Mob to Allow Secretaries to Whack People

Female grunt: He gets all the good assignments! I had to spell, he gets to shoot people!

*9th Street, Sheldon, Iowa*


## Checking Back in with the Department of Redundancy Department

Coworker #1: What is our vision statement?
Coworker #2: It says here, "Our vision is to always be true to our vision."

*101 South Webster Street, Madison, Wisconsin*


## Refuses to Watch Baseball Because of the Flies

Suit: The other way I learned it, from Schoolhouse Rock, is that the alligator is hungry and so wants to bite the larger one.
Woman coworker: *Ohhh* . . . I see. That would confuse me because it's got animals.

*919 3rd Avenue, New York, New York*


## When the Company Switched to Voodoo Performance Management

Coworker #1: What the hell am I looking at here?
Coworker #2: Could be blood, could be nothing.

*Alpharetta, Georgia*

## Who Can't See Their Fingers

Office grunt #1: Ha! They have phones with big numbers for people with fat fingers.
Office grunt #2: Don't be mean—they're probably for deaf people.

*25 North Terrace, Adelaide, Australia*

## What Can I Say? It Gets His Wife Hot.

Coworker on phone: You'd be an amazing human being if you brought me some nibbles on your way here. If not, then you're clearly the Mongoloid I always suspected you to be.

*401 West Clarendon Avenue, Phoenix, Arizona*

## Thus, He Probably Overcharged for His Chuppahs

Drone #1: Well, we already live together.
Drone #2: Oooh, living in sin!
Drone #3: Jesus won't be happy with you.
Drone #1: Well, I'm Jewish, so Jesus already isn't too happy with me.
Drone #3: That's true.
Drone #1: I think when I get married under a chuppah he might get upset!
Drone #2: Jesus was Jewish, though.
Drone #3: Jesus was also a carpenter.

*1500 Broadway, New York, New York*

## Even His Core Constituency Is Turning on Him

Intern: When is Bush's last term?
Employee: Um, right now. It ends in '08.
Intern: Good, 'cause he's stupid.

*1065 Williams Street, Atlanta, Georgia*

## You Can Lead a Horse to a Basket of Eggs, but You Can't Make a Silk Purse Out of a Pig in a Poke

Clerk watching two inexperienced clerks trying to help each other: That's like the dog leading the blind.

*South Lamar Street, Roxboro, North Carolina*

## The Best Way to Try Something New Is to Maintain at Least a Little Connection to the Familiar

Chick #1: You know that gay guy that works second shift?
Chick #2: Yeah, what about him?
Chick #1: I took him out to meet all my hetero friends, and they enjoyed the shit out of him.

*2800 East 28th Street, Minneapolis, Minnesota*

## He Bought It from This Little Old Lady Who Said She Had Trouble with Flooding

Female coworker: My uncle just bought a condom in Brooklyn. It's a real nice place.
Male coworker: Really?

Female coworker: Uh-huh.

*99 Church Street, New York, New York*


## When Art History Majors Enter the Workforce

Admin #1: There is a 30 percent chance that it will rain today.

Admin #2: Wow! That means there is a 60 percent chance that it won't.

*6606 Tussing Road, Reynoldsburg, Ohio*


## Mmm, As Long As Their Robot Digits Have Speed Settings . . .

Cube dweller #1: Stupid fucking Back Office Support people are *retarded*.

Cube dweller #2: Fuck the fucking fuckers.

Cube dweller #1: *Amen* . . . Without the sex part . . .

Cube dweller #2: Heh, their pillow talk would go something like this: "You are the one that is hot, that is what I am telling you now."

*1601 Bryan Street, Dallas, Texas*


## You Also Need to Have Finished Third-Grade Math

Worker: Yup, it takes a lot more than a million dollars to be a millionaire these days.

*Hermiston, Oregon*

## As an Engineering Major He Wasn't Required to Know Where He Was

Office peon #1: So this U Mass . . . That in Mass?

Office peon #2: Yeah.

Office peon #1: Is this "Mass" a city?

Office peon #2: Nah, more like a town.

*Berkshires, Massachusetts*


## It's Funny, Though—There's This One Where Everyone Has a Four-Year Sentence

Intern chick: Where's Ithaca?

Bronx boy: It's upstate.

Intern chick: Upstate?

Bronx boy: Way upstate.

Intern chick: So, where are we?

Bronx boy: We're southern—the very southern tip of New York.

Intern chick: Okay, how far north is it?

Bronx boy: Really far north . . . It's near prisons, if you really want to know the truth.

*125th Street & Lenox Avenue, New York, New York*


## She's Either Got a Really Short Spine or Is Crouching on Her Heels

Male coworker: What are those? Are they thighs?

Female coworker: No, they're breasts. Gi-normous breasts!

*555 West 57th Street, New York, New York*

## And If They Show Up Here, I Called in Sick, Okay?

Employee: Hey, Kathy*! I was so happy to see you come to
work this morning!

Kathy: Yup, the police didn't pick me up! Whew!

*Swiss chalet near Highway 401, Whitby, Ontario, Canada*

## The Truth Is Just Too Explosive

Female coworker #1: I just don't know what to tell my kid.

Female coworker #2: What about?

Female coworker #1: Well, my six-year-old wants to know
what's the difference between a lamb and a sheep.

Female coworker #2: Oh, that's tough. What are you going
to tell her?

Female coworker #1: I dunno, probably that they are just
similar species.

*South Research Place, Central Islip, New York*

## Luckily, All the Prejudice Is Concentrated in Mississippi, Where We Can Keep an Eye on It

Receptionist: You should move to Mississippi so your children won't have to go to school with all those black
kids. . . . But people in Mississippi are really prejudiced,
though. . . .

*Memphis, Tennessee*

## You Should See the Water Sports Department

Female coworker: What are Dick's?
Male coworker: Oh, Dick's are huge!

*Minneapolis, Minnesota*


## It's Right Next to That Note That Says You Should Give Me All Your Money

Office peon #1: Hey, what budget number should we use for this? The old one or the new one?
Office peon #2: What does that email you printed out and pinned to your wall say?
Office peon #1: It says I should use the new one.
Office peon #2: Then I think you should use the new one.
Office peon #1: Cool, thanks!
Office peon #2: No problem.

*5201 Paint Branch Parkway, College Park, Maryland*


## Nothing in the KGB's Training Had Prepared Colonel Volkov for the Mystery of American Names

IT person: Usually the email address is just the first initial, then the employee's last name.
Salesguy: Oh, okay . . . What's John Smith's* last name, again?

*Columbia, South Carolina*

### . . . In the Chair. I Think We're Paying Him So He Doesn't Kill Us.

Salesman: Yeah, I'm fucking fed up with that guy. He hasn't sent in his reports for weeks—just keeps flying out to Texas. What the fuck are we paying him for, anyway?

Manager: Texas? What's he doing in Texas?

Salesman: Oh, apparently his dad died or something.

*3000 Birch Street, Brea, California*

### Taking the "Vice" Out of "Sleeping with the Vice President" One Rationalization at a Time

Woman #1: He had such a big penis.

Woman #2: Oh my god, that is so hot. Did you hear about Richard*?

Woman #1: But he is a subordinate! I am not cheating on my husband with a subordinate. It feels more guilty that way. At least I feel like I'm gaining more than pleasure from sleeping with the exec.

*Main Street, Cambridge, Massachusetts*

### And You're "About" the Most Intelligent Woman I've Ever Met

Male coworker: Check out this photo.

Female coworker: This is an old photo of you.

Male coworker: Yeah, it was taken around 1991.

Female coworker: Wow! That was about twenty-seven years ago!

*6606 Tussing Road, Reynoldsburg, Ohio*

## Only Bitter Experience Prompts This Kind of Advice

Rep on phone with trucker: You do know you can't drive your rig into the ocean, right? That's bad . . . Oh, okay. Well, I hope you have a nice view!

*1368 Old Fannin Road, Brandon, Mississippi*


## Define "Okay"

IT chick: We're upgrading the database on Tuesday morning. Is that okay with your schedule?
Admin: I'm out on Tuesday.
IT chick: Because the office manager says Tuesday afternoon is better for her, so we may need to do it in the afternoon.
Admin: I'm out on Tuesday.
IT chick: But the morning is better for the advisor, so we're going to try to do it on Tuesday morning.
Admin: I'm out on Tuesday.
IT chick: So is Tuesday okay?

*University, Florida*


## Dwayne Suffers from Premature Evaluation

Secretary: Would you like to go out sometime?
Peon: I've already dated you, slept with you, and broken up with you in my head. There's really no need.

*Denver, Colorado*

## Tupac, Perchance to Dream

White girl clerk: If I were a rapper my name would be "Big Tupac" and people would hate me.

*2930 Grants Lake Boulevard, Houston, Texas*

## Immoral *and* Fattening? No Fair!

Secretary #1: What are you going to be for Halloween?

Secretary #2: I don't believe in Halloween. Pumpkins are evil. They are from the devil.

Secretary #3: Didn't you bring pumpkin pie to the Christmas party last year?

Secretary #1: Pumpkins for Christmas are okay, I guess. Jesus loves those pumpkins.

Secretary #2, mumbling: Y'all goin' to hell.

*University of South Florida, Tampa, Florida*

## Cause of Death: Self-Inflicted Shipping Error

Male coworker: Henry,* Mary* is going to kill you this time! Who shipped this?

Henry: Mary.

Male coworker: Mary committed suicide!

*6105 Oakleaf Avenue, Baltimore, Maryland*

## Always Sandwich Criticism Between Two Compliments

Coworker #1, staring at a can full of pens: Where are all the pens?

Coworker #2: You have pretty hair.

*Colorado Springs, Colorado*


## Haven't You Found the Controls Yet?

Office guy #1: You have been snippish today.
Office chick: Well, I haven't had sex for about three months.
Office guy #2: Break out the phone numbers!
Office chick: What I need is a good, old-fashioned fucking to relieve the tension.

*Clarksville, Tennessee*


## Inseminated Grandma Through Two Nightshirts and a Copy of the London *Times*

Lady entering office: God, it's as hot as my grandpa's balls in here!

*Maiden Lane, San Francisco, California*


## Come on . . . "Large-Mouth" Bass?

Young office peon: What did you do this weekend?
Old office peon: My son and I tried going fishing. . . . It was really something.
Young office peon: Oh, yeah?
Old office peon: We were getting blown everywhere.

*York Street, New Haven, Connecticut*

## We Usually Only Hire Employees Who Can Be Eradicated with Penicillin

Employee: How long are you working with us?
Intern: I'm never leaving. I'm like a bad STD.

*420 Lexington Avenue, New York, New York*


## Paradoxically, He Just Talked About Them

Male lunch breaker #1: So, she gave me this look like she'd do things to me that I could never talk about.
Male lunch breaker #2: Like what?
Male lunch breaker #1: I'm not sure, but it would probably involve chocolate syrup, handcuffs, lots of leather, and a ball-gag.
Female lunch breaker: Those things make it hard to breathe.

*910 Louisiana Avenue, Houston, Texas*


## Watch Out! They Spit!

Colleague #1: I'm having a yak attack.
Colleague #2: You're being assaulted by a Himalayan beast of burden?
Colleague #1: Cognac. Cognac. When you want cognac it means you're having a yak attack.
Colleague #2: I didn't know Himalayan beasts of burden drank alcohol.
Colleague #1: They do if I'm buyin'!
Colleague #3: What are you guys even talking about?

Colleague #4: Oh, ignore them. They want to get drunk with camels or something.

*4300 Amon Carter Boulevard, Fort Worth, Texas*

## Even If It Sucked, That Movie Would Still Be Working Here

Cube dweller #1: Hey, if someone on the Atkins Diet turned into a zombie, would bread repel them?

Cube dweller #2: What do you mean?

Cube dweller #1: Well, zombies usually continue doing tasks they did before they were re-animated. They're afraid of bread . . . so do you think if someone on the Atkins Diet turned into a zombie you could cover yourself in bread and other tasty carb-filled foods and you'd be safe?

Cube dweller #2: I don't know, but we should totally turn that into a movie!

*9495 Harvard Boulevard, Youngstown, Ohio*

## Bigfoot

Partner: If he had a fifteen-inch dick you'd want to know. . . .

Office girl: Right.

Partner: I mean, come on—fifteen inches. That's like a foot!

*Wacker Drive, Chicago, Illinois*

### He'll Fit Right In

Office girl #1: So, what are you snacking on?
Office girl #2: [Muffled.] . . . Cock . . .
Office girl #3: Whose?
Manager on open intercom: Oh my god! You're gonna scare away the new guy!
Office girl #1: What's his name?
Office girl #2: [Muffled.] . . . Dick . . .

*Hagerstown, Maryland*

### No, You Fools! The East! The East!

Office grunt: They are the only ones I know who could fuck up a sunrise.

*357 Carpenter Street, Ontario, Canada*

### It's This (Removes Pants)

Guy worker #1: I want to ride a missile. I think that'd be the best way to go—just riding a missile.
Girl worker: Go where?
Guy worker #2: *Die!*
Girl worker: Oh . . . What's a missile?

*Cape May, New Jersey*

### Some Guys Have All the Luck

Gay coworker: I'm dead fussy about my sausages. . . . [Office laughs.] No, I mean sausages to eat!

*Sauchiehall Street, Glasgow, Scotland*

## Sometimes You Don't Know Whether to Be Happy or Sad, or Even for Whom

Worker bee: Well, you know, I won that really soft pillow here yesterday at the celebration, but I just took it home and gave it to my dog to hump.

*14840 Conference Center Drive, Chantilly, Virginia*


## The Rest of the Windshield Is Just Fine

Coworker #1: How much does a new windshield cost?
Coworker #2: I don't know, but I'll let you know. . . .
Coworker #3: Are they replacing the whole windshield?
Coworker #2: No, only the crack.

*Lanham, Maryland*


## She Helps Mr. Patinkin Pretend He's Straight

Office girl #1, lunching on grass: My mandarin is the worst mandarin I've ever eaten.
Office girl #2: That sucks.
Office girl #1: But it's kinda good. . . . Look! I can use it to put the pips in, like a bowl! I could wear it as a beard!
Office girl #1: You're a *mandybeard*!

*450 St. Kilda Road, Melbourne, Australia*


## Well, White People Are the New Hippies

White chick worker: I went to dinner with my dad last night.
Mexican guy worker: Oh, yeah? Where?

White chick worker: We went to Souplantation. It's like HomeTown Buffet, but for white people.

Asian guy worker: I thought Souplantation was the Home-Town Buffet for hippies.

*Agoura Hills, California*


## Why Texas Is Known as the Pros State

Female coworker: Are you going to donate five dollars for Jeans Day?

Male coworker: Depends, what's the five bucks go to?

Female coworker: Breast cancer research.

Male coworker: Lame. What about prostate cancer?

Female coworker: You're a guy! You should want to save boobs!

Male coworker: Not old cancer boobs. Besides, if my prostate is shot, what's the point?

Female coworker: You're going to hell.

*910 Louisiana Street, Houston, Texas*


## Sure, Just Get 'Em a Case of Beer

Secretary #1, noticing cable grommet at computer desk: Jesus Christ! Is your hole bigger?

Secretary #2: Yeah, maintenance came in over the weekend and reamed it out.

Secretary #1: Think they'd do mine?

*3379 Jackson Street, Kansas City, Missouri*

## They Belong Just Outside

Office grunt: Oh, don't get your panties in a twat!

*Springfield, Missouri*


## Why It's Called "Software"

Coworker: Here, let me show you. I just have to get it up.

*Houston, Texas*


## Woulda Called in Sick, but I Needed a Rest

Employee: Man, my arm is sore as hell from playing with my Wii all weekend.

*Oltorf Road, Austin, Texas*


## But Two Years Later She and Tom Cruise Are Still Together

Cube dweller about submitting an invoice: I'm going to just do him and get him out of the way.

*164 Summit Avenue, Providence, Rhode Island*


## Or Is It Me? I Can Never Remember.

Cube dweller on phone with wife: You think I'm the idiot, you fucking idiot? You're the idiot! . . . No! I said you're the idiot! . . . No! I said you're the idiot. . . . What?! No, I'm not the idiot, you're the idiot! We both know you're the idiot. I gotta go. We both know who the idiot is. You are

the idiot. Dinner? . . . Okay, I'll bring it to you. . . . Okay. . . .
No, you're still the idiot. . . . Okay, you're right. I love you.
Bye. [Hangs up, muttering.] She is such an idiot. . . .

*St. Louis, Missouri*

## Without Additional Data

Male coworker: I think I hit myself on the side. It hurts.
Female coworker: So pull up your shirt and let me see!
Male coworker: [Silence.]
Female coworker: Pull up your shirt! I'm not gonna rape ya!

*1250 Broadway, New York, New York*

## Sounds Dumb Until You Learn It's February 29

Bartender #1: I can't believe I'll be thirty soon!
Bartender #2: It's okay, your birthday will come and go. . . .
Bartender #3: Oh, your birthday is coming up? When is it?
This year?!

*1 Frank Sinatra Drive, Hoboken, New Jersey*

## What about *My* Needs?

Customer service rep: Seriously, get off my face!

*333 South 7th Street, Minneapolis, Minnesota*

## When the Company Outing Went Sour

Coworker: Yeah. Strip clubs—not good . . . But dolphins are
okay!

*2323 West 38th Street, Erie, Pennsylvania*

## Dave: We're Selling It to the Gypsies, Why Get Attached?

Coworker #1: Dave* was in with his new baby. I asked him her name, and he didn't know.

Coworker #2: Isn't it Emma*? [Coworker #1 nods.] *I* knew it and I'm not even the baby's daddy. . . . I don't think. . . .

*Des Moines, Iowa*


## Poor Fellow—He's Taking His Mother's Death Pretty Hard

Male coworker: Look! I'm Bambi! [Jumps over moving conveyor belt.] Wheee! The *meadooowww*!

*1800 Ward Avenue, West Chester, Pennsylvania*


## What Are Your Design Tolerances?

Engineer #1: I'm kind of anal about how that's done.

Engineer #2: Well, permit me to offend your anal side for a moment. . . .

*East Harmony Road, Fort Collins, Colorado*


## Maintenance: Well, *There's* Your Problem, Sir

Annoying office mate: Oh my god! It's big! It's *huuuge*! Oh my god, it's in my crack!

*Pittsburgh, Pennsylvania*

## Divinyls: When I Think About Work I Touch My Area

Woman #1: I'm having trouble with my area today.

Woman #2: What? I don't need to know about your area.

Woman #1: No, you sicko—my work area. Everything I touch today is breaking! What did you think I meant?

Woman #2: Oh, never mind.

*Main Street, Louisville, Kentucky*


## She Woke Up Thirty Pounds Heavier and with Syphilis This Morning

Female coworker: I just got dumped by a text message!

Male coworker: Ouch! You just got K-Feded!

*Monument Circle, Indianapolis, Indiana*


## We Give and Give of Our Urine, and What Thanks Do We Get?

Male colleague to boss: So, the urinals aren't flushing again. . . . I really think we need to get the landlord in to fix that. I mean, we've held up our end. . . .

*Ad agency, Berlin Mitte, Germany*


## If He Pulls Your Hair, It Means He Likes You

Man brushes past pretty woman on his way out of an elevator and growls loudly.

Startled woman: Did he just *growl* at me?

Male coworker: Yes!

Female coworker: Yeah, it didn't sound like he was just clearing his throat.

Startled woman: I thought so!

Male coworker: Maybe he was just growling at you to get you to move. You know, like, "*Grrr!* Get *out* of my *way*!"

*Elevator, 710 2nd Avenue, Seattle, Washington*

## If You Really Want It to Stick to Things, Yes

Coworker planning baby shower: You think I should spend sixty bucks on Butt Paste?!

*4803 Deer Lake Drive, Jacksonville, Mississippi*

## Wait, Which One Is the Pothead?

Pothead intern: Do you smoke? You know, like weed?

Midtwenties employee: Not as much as I when I first graduated.

Pothead intern: Oh, really?

Midtwenties employee: Yeah, like maybe once or twice—

Pothead intern: A month?

Midtwenties employee: Oh, no, man—a week.

*Framingham, Massachusetts*

## Hey, Don't Laugh—with Reproductive Tech the Way It Is, This Is Only a Few Years Away

Female coworker to another: You're my stud!

*Seattle, Washington*

## I Dunno—Can You Cluck Like a Chicken?

Coworker #1: Is Sue* in town?

Coworker #2: No, she'll be back in two weeks.

Coworker #1: Damn.

Coworker #2: Why? Do you want me to be her?

*3201 West Commercial Boulevard, Fort Lauderdale, Florida*

## And If You Hear Anything Outside the Office Door, *Do Not* Open It

Guy #1: You staying till ten tonight?

Guy #2: Yeah.

Guy #1: Then let me explain the procedures to you. First of all, you leave at ten. . . .

*Barger & Echo Hollow, Eugene, Oregon*

## A More Relevant Question Would Have Been, "Where Will I Put This?"

Coworker with camera cord in hand, confused: Where do I put this?

Officemate: Anywhere you want to, baby.

*Frances Avenue, Lancaster, Pennsylvania*

## It Was Asking for It, Though

Lady: I just called the vending machine a cunt rag . . . I don't think I've ever done that before in my life.

*Varick & Canal Streets, New York, New York*

## Starting on Blurgsday

Office grunt #1: So, when are you going to take your vacation?

Office grunt #2: Well, seeing as how Thanksgiving falls on a Sunday this year. . . .

*Richardson, Texas*


## But I Pay for More Expensive Hookers

Office peon: Does it itch? When I do it a lot mine itches.

*2717 Arlington Road, Akron, Ohio*


## He Just Ordered a Pizza

Lady cube dweller: Well, didn't you get bigger last time?

Man cube dweller: Yeah, but I was thinking about something else.

Lady cube dweller: What were you thinking about?!

Man cube dweller: Your sister.

Lady cube dweller: You're an asshole.

Man cube dweller: Well, she *is* my girlfriend.

*4015 Shore Drive, Indianapolis, Indiana*


## What about Tube Steak?

Staffer #1: Do you want to grab some lunch?

Staffer #2: I don't eat French fries.

*Austin, Texas*

coworkers

**131**

## When He Sees the Seventh Posture of the Perfumed Garden, It's Time to Stop

Employee #1: My fiancé is colorblind, and they found out when he was young because he would color things the wrong colors.

Employee #2: How does he drive? He can't tell which color means Go and which one means Stop!

Employee #1, perplexed: He memorizes the positions.

*North Rocky Point Drive, Tampa, Florida*


## I Stand Up Straighter, Too, When Someone Holds My Shaft

Coworker #1: You really need to be concerned about the angle and the length of the shaft and how it meets the head.

Coworker #2: Oh, yeah?

Coworker #1: It's fairly stiff, and the shaft just flows straight into the head. When I hold it right, the top of it comes here, it makes me stand up straight.

*222 Severn Avenue, Annapolis, Maryland*


## The Barter Economy Starts with Essentials

Sales girl: Oooh, that's fancy-schmancy. What'd you have to do to get that?

Sales guy, not missing a beat: Blow job.

*England Street, Charlotte, North Carolina*

## Dating Tip #298: This Pickup Line Works with "X-Box," "Bread-Box," and "Sandbox" as Well

Coworker, sarcastically: Oh, my inbox is so much fun right now. Who wants to come play in my inbox? Who wants to come play?

*300 Crescent Court, Dallas, Texas*

((( **customers**

## It's the Fifty-First!

Clerk: Ma'am, I can't take this money.

Lady: Why not? It's good American money.

Clerk: Ma'am, this money is from Canada.

Lady: Is Canada not the fiftieth state of the U.S., or are you stupid or something?

Clerk: I'm not the one that's stupid.

*13697 West Colonial Drive, Winter Garden, Florida*

## And What Could I Cover It With?

Customer: What's this called?

Sales associate: A duvet cover.

Customer: No, no . . . What's inside it?

Sales associate: A duvet.

*Furniture store, Costa Mesa, California*

## I Wondered What James Stockdale Was Up to These Days

Operator: Thank you for calling Bayshore Medical Insurance;* how can I assist?

Caller: So, who are you?

Operator: We're an insurance company.

Caller: And what do you do?

Operator: We help you with your insurance.

Caller: I don't understand.

Operator: Well, your boss gives you benefits for working there, and our job is to help you use your benefits.

Caller: I don't have any benefits! I never signed up for this! Did my boss tell you to call me? Is he trying to set me up? Who told you to call me?

Operator: Sir, *you* called *me*.

*Market Street, San Francisco, California*


## But You Can Pour This Cappuccino in Your Underpants

Customer: Yes, I'd like a grande Dolce and Gabbana latte . . .

Extremely patient barista: You mean a Dolce cinnamon latte?

Customer: *No!* I said Dolce and Gabbana, and that's what I want!

Extremely patient barista: I'm sorry, ma'am, we don't sell that here anymore.

*Starbucks, Indian River Road, Virginia Beach, Virginia*


## Just a Little One That Will Change the Way I See Things

Female customer: My sunglasses are broken. One of the screws fell out, and a guy in here yesterday said they would replace them with a new pair.

Woman behind counter: Oh, I remember you. You're just looking for a screw, right?

Female customer: Aren't we all, really?

*1051 North Rush Street, Chicago, Illinois*

### He Should Ask to Speak to a Buddhist CSR, Fluent in the Language of Reincarnation

Heated caller: So, let me understand this—if I die, I get a hundred thousand dollars?

Customer service rep: No. If you pass, your beneficiary will receive a hundred thousand dollars.

Heated caller: But it's my money. I am paying the premium for it. I should be able to get my money. Why can't I have my money?!

Customer service rep: Because you will be dead, ma'am.

Heated caller: That's ridiculous. I want to speak with a manager.

*1 Sartan Way, Merrimack, New Hampshire*


### Right Next to the "Irony" Button

Customer trying to use his debit card: I gotta push "English"? "Spanish" shouldn't be an option. If they can't speak no English, they ain't got no business being here. Where's the "Yes" button at?

Cashier: It's the button that says "Yes" on it.

*Grocery store, Roanoke, Virginia*


### So Many Jobs Are Made Interesting Only by the Arbitrary Exercise of Petty Authority

Customer service rep: I'll be right with you, ma'am. He was first.

Female customer: No, he wasn't.

Customer service rep: Yes, he was.

Male customer: No, I wasn't.

Customer service rep: Yes, you were.

*Bank, New York, New York*

## Just Take It! What's He Going to Do, Tell You You're Shoplifting?

Customer: I'm looking for one of those things where I can plug it into my TV's video and plug like four video game systems into it and push a button to switch between them.

Employee: Yeah, I don't think we sell those.

Customer, picking up item: I'm looking for this.

Employee: Oh, we don't sell those.

Customer: You . . . don't . . . sell these?

Employee: No.

Customer: You're sure?

Employee: Yeah, we definitely don't sell those.

Customer: You don't sell these? This thing that I picked up off your rack with a price tag on it?

Employee: No. XYZ Company* might carry them, though.

*Electronics store, Astoria, New York*

## That's Hardly a Reason. He Must Have Smelled Bad.

Customer: I would like to complain about the woman who works here. She was very rude to me for no reason, even yelling, and then made me leave.

139

Clerk: Are you the guy who was walking around naked?

Customer: Oh . . . Ah, well . . . [Leaves quickly.]

*Porn store, Bozeman, Montana*

## Yes, in Prairie Schooners

Travel agent: Where were you looking to take a cruise to?

Client: Do they have cruises to Las Vegas?

*Proctor Street, Tacoma, Washington*

## Can We All Agree That What They Do Is Not "Acting"?

Client #1: Yeah . . . [My girlfriend] used to be an actress.

Client #2, looking at photo on Client #1's desk: Yeah? I think I have seen her before.

Client #1: Yeah? You watch a lot of porn? She used to be a porn actress.

Client #2: [Silence.]

*Airport Plaza, Long Beach, California*

## They Stopped Doing the Circular Because of the Weird Envelopes

Customer: Do you have a circular for this week?

Cashier: Uh, no. We don't have those.

Customer: You don't have a flyer advertising your weekly specials?

Cashier: Oh, you mean *this*?

Customer: Yeah! The circular. What I said.

Cashier: Ma'am, this is not a circular. This is a rectangle.

*Clothing store, Waldorf, Maryland*

## He's Also Been Divorced for Three Years but Doesn't Know It

Client: Why do I have financial charges? It was a plan for "same as cash" for eighteen months.

Customer service rep: Well, sir, we sent you eighteen months of statements telling you that if you don't pay by the due date, you'll have financial charges to pay and exactly how much they would be.

Client: You expected me to read my mail?

*Bank, Toronto, Ontario, Canada*

## The Colombians Were Bidding Higher When the Market Closed

Receptionist: Thank you for calling Widgets, Inc.* How may I help you?

Customer: I got a letter from my insurance company telling me to fill out a paper with my social security number on it and send it to you. Who are you?

Receptionist: We work with the government to help you with your appeal.

Customer: Oh. So you won't be selling my social security number to anybody in Nigeria?

Receptionist: No, sir, not today.

*50 Square Drive, Rochester, New York*

## What Happens When a Tourist Is Deaf to All Parts of Speech Except Nouns

Tourist: What is this special wine deal you have tonight?

Waitress: Well, it's five-dollar Italian wine night, so any wine that is made in Italy is five dollars. But we are out of Sauvignon Blanc and Pinot Grigio.

Tourist: Well, I guess I'll have a glass of Sauvignon Blanc.

Waitress: We're out of that. Anything else?

Tourist: Then I'll have a glass of Pinot Grigio.

*17th & P Streets, Washington, DC*

## She Made the Same Mistake with Love in the 1960s

Technician: Ma'am, your Jaguar needs a new engine.

Jag owner: How can that be?

Technician: When's the last time you had the oil changed?

Jag owner: My salesperson, Vinnie,* told me the car was maintenance-free, and just bring it in when it needs service.

Technician: No, ma'am, it's not maintenance-free, it's free maintenance.

*1815 Maplelawn Drive, Troy, Michigan*

## Charging Extra for Stupidity Could Turn the Country's Finances Around in a Year or Two

Intercom: Welcome to Fast Food, Inc.* Can I take your order?

Woman: Yes, I'd like a Number Two with a Sprite, please.

Intercom: That will be $8.43 . . . Mild or spicy?

Woman: Yes.

Intercom: Mild or spicy?

Woman: Yes, please.

Intercom: [Laughter.]

Woman: What? What?

Intercom: That will be $41.23.

*Waldorf, Maryland*


## I Just *Hate* Being Held Accountable for My Actions

Customer service rep: Thanks for calling Stuff, Inc.* How may I help you?

Client on phone: Yeah, I was just talking to Roger,* and we lost connection. Maybe you can finish walking me through whatever.

Customer service rep: Sir, we do not have a Roger. You were just talking to me. We didn't lose connection. You hung up on me, and I was walking you through understanding that our software does not do "whatever."

*8th floor, Galleria, Hoover, Alabama*


## Learn to See Delay as a Gift of Time

Tech: Are you all set on the PDF server now?

Client: Yes, I think so. Is it supposed to be so fucking slow uploading PDFs onto the FTP site?

Tech: Yup! That's a feature.

Client: Neat. Thanks.

*111 South 1st Avenue, Wausau, Wisconsin*

## Things Don't Always Go Smoothly at Karl Rove's House

Customer service rep: Okay, let's take a look at the installation instructions.

Customer: You mean that little book? That looked like documentation, so I threw it away.

*Fairfax, Virginia*

## Do the Math? *Do the Math?* You Can't *Handle* the Math!

Customer: They're three for ninety-nine cents.

Cashier: We don't sell them at that price. They're thirty-three cents each.

*Discount store, 498 South Boulder Highway, Henderson, Nevada*

## No, You've Just Got Those Little Wings on Your Lapel

Customer: By chance, was your mom a flight attendant?

Employee: Why, do you think you're my dad?

*Costa Mesa, California*

## Oh, Okay. Tweetie.

Teen girl holding bag with dead bird inside: My grandfather called earlier about getting this bird checked for West Nile virus. He found it in his yard.

Office clerk: Okay, I remember talking to him this morning. I
    need to get some information from you, first. Now, what
    was his name?

The girl's eyes go wide, and she looks at the bag.

Office clerk: No, not the bird's name. I need to know your
    grandfather's name.

*616 Court Street, Oberlin, Louisiana*

## Shopping at Tautology

Girl: Excuse me, do you carry tonic water?
Stock boy: Yeah, I think so. I mean, if we have it it's proba-
    bly somewhere in the store.
Girl: Uh, thanks.

*Grocery store, Memphis, Tennessee*

## Just a Minute—I'll Czech

Customer: Hi, can I get hold of Czech crowns here?
Bank flunky: Uhhh . . . What was his first name, again?

*Bank, Great North Road, Auckland, New Zealand*

## Who's on (Safety) First?

Receptionist: Hello! Thank you for calling Avon* Safety,
    where safety comes first. How may I direct your call?
Voice #1: How do I direct the call?
Voice #2: [Indecipherable.]

Voice #1: I don't know. That's all it says. . . .

Receptionist: Hello? This is not a recording.

Voice #1: She said it's a recording.

Receptionist: No! This is not a recording! Hello?

Voice #1: What do I do?

Voice #2: Hang up. [Hangs up.]

*Avon, Massachusetts*


## Those Will Cost Extra to Remove

Painter in room with painter's tape everywhere: Do you like the new colors?

Customer: I don't like the blue stripes.

*Concord, New Hampshire*


## Sir, You Need More Services Than I Can Provide

Customer service rep: Okay, sir, go ahead and click on the logo in the top left of your screen.

Customer: I don't see that. I'm on a page that says, "Welcome," then, "My Profile."

Customer service rep: Okay, go ahead and click on "My Profile."

Customer: I don't see that.

*9800 Fredericksburg Road, San Antonio, Texas*


## Thought I'd Rob Your Punk Ass, Is Why

Employee: Can I help you find something?

Customer: No, you don't have it.

Employee: Then why are you still here?

## Lame Duck Car Buyers

Old woman: How dare you pick me up in a truck? I drive a
    Cadillac, and you pick me up in a truck?! This is the last
    Cadillac I ever buy from you!
Manager: That's not much of a threat, now, is it?
    Seriously—look at you. I mean, there's not a lot of Cadil-
    lacs left in you, is there?

*Car dealership, Ohio*


## This Turkey Baster Says You Are Mistaken

Coworker: My wife's not too happy with me.
Client: Oh, I'm sure—
Coworker: No, she's pregnant again.
Client: Oooh, that's gotta be your fault. No woman would do
    that to herself.

*Highland Avenue, Cheshire, Connecticut*


## God: I'd Like to Return This Woman, Please

Customer: Hi, I'd like to make a return.
Cashier: Okay, do you have your receipt?
Customer: Yeah, here it is.
Cashier, after looking at receipt for a few seconds: Ma'am,
    this is from Walgreens.

Customer: Oh . . . [Looks around the store in bewilder-
ment.] Where am I?

*Drugstore, Livermore, California*


## You Have to Keep Your Pinkie Extended

Customer: I have not ordered this product.

Service person: But we have a contract that you have
signed.

Customer: How do you think it feels if I rape you in your ass
every month?

Service person: I'm sorry?

Customer: How do you think it feels if I rape you in your ass
every month?

Service person: Would you do it like a gentleman?

*Potsdam, Germany*


## We Tell Them Americans Are Fat Monsters. Is That What You Meant?

Trainer: In America, when our kids don't finish their meals
we tell them that there are starving kids in Africa. What
do you tell them?

Kenyan clients: [Silence.]

*Cafeteria, 258 Monrovia Street, Nairobi, Kenya*


## Fool! The Customer Is Always Right!

Customer: Hello, Janice,* how are you today?

Worker: I'm not Janice, I'm Sue.*

Customer: Your name tag says *Janice*.

Worker: No, it doesn't. It says *Sue*, see? J-A-N . . . Oops! Wrong name tag . . .

*Westmoreland Mall, Greensburg, Pennsylvania*

## It's Always Happy Hour Somewhere

Admin: I'm sorry, that person has left for the day. We close at 5 p.m.

Caller: Well, it's only a little after four here, so does that mean that I, like, have to call you in your time zone?

Admin: Uh, well, yes. Yes, you do. . . .

*Mount Desert Island, Maine*

## Cat Burglars and Ninjas Have Ruined Blackness for Everyone

Black guy: What would you say if I said I wanted to get a Mystic Tan?

Tanning consultant: Oh, you could. It would give you a nice glow.

Black guy: You're not even going to discourage me?! I would never get a spray-on tan. The blacker you are the higher people assume your crime rate is.

*North 222 Plaza, Reading, Pennsylvania*

## The Last Event He Remembers Clearly Is V-J Day

Old man: Excuse me.

Employee: Yes.

Old man: Where do you keep your Negro music?
Employee: What?
Old man: Your Negro music!
Grandson: He means rap music.
Employee: Oh, over there.

*CD store, 1st Avenue North, Seattle, Washington*


## They Prefer to Be Called . . . Um . . . Something Different This Year

Older woman #1: What are you going to do while you're here?
Young man: Oh, I'm gonna shop like a mofo!
Older woman #1: "Mofo"? What is that?
Older woman #2: What does that mean?
Young man: Uh . . . It, uh . . . means I'm gonna shop *a lot*!
Older woman #2: Oh . . . Is that a Negro term?

*Victoria, British Columbia, Canada*


## Astonished at His Success, the Customer Went on to Broker Peace Between the Israelis and the Palestinians

Employee: Hi, can I help you?
Customer: Yes, I'd like a dinner for twelve, please.
Employee: Oh, I'm sorry. For orders that large you have to call catering at least twenty-four hours in advance.
Customer: Er, then how about two dinners for six?
Employee: Oh, sure, we can do that.

*Take-out restaurant, Highway 60 & Limona Road, Brandon, Florida*

## He Means It's Inauthentically Trying to Be Like Soup Without Actually Being Soup

Customer: Excuse me, miss!

Waitress: Yes, sir?

Customer: My soup is too soupy.

Waitress: Well, I'm sorry, sir, if your soup is too soupy, but it *is* soup.

*Point Pleasant, New Jersey*

## Sure, Just Wad It Up So It Fits Through Those Little Holes in the Phone

Customer: Do I have to pay for that over the phone?

Customer service rep: Yes, ma'am.

Customer: Do you take cash?

*Glenwood Avenue, Raleigh, North Carolina*

## News Flash: Truce Ending Hundred Years' War Shattered!

Telephone customer: Hi, I need to find the international rates for calling to France.

Local phone operator: France? That's in England, right?

*55 Water Street, New York, New York*

## We're Still Trying to Get the Pope to Stop Using the Abacus

Techie: I'm sorry about the delay. We're using a new system, and I liked the old system. I'm a creature of habit and resist change.

Customer: Tell me about it—I'm with the Archdiocese.

*555 International Way, Springfield, Oregon*

## The Quality-Control Spies Never Catch Anyone with This Question

Customer: Do you sell cards?

Hallmark employee: Yes. Yes, we do.

*Hallmark store, Manhattan, Kansas*

## Lottery Board: Eeexcellent!

Customer: These ice cream cones and a hundred dollars in lotto tickets.

Store clerk: Okay, $106.39

Customer: What? These ice creams cost six dollars?! What a waste of money! No, I don't want them. What a waste. Seriously! No, no—just the lotto tickets.

*Eastlake Market, Seattle, Washington*

## After Emptying the Register, the Robbers Attempted to Unsuccessfully Masquerade as Employees

Employee: Can I help you?

Customer: Hi. Yes, may I have a turkey artichoke panini?

Employee: No.

Customer: No?

Employee: No. We don't have those.

Customer: But it's right there on your board. Do you mean you ran out of them today?

Employee: Yeah, that's what I said. Order the other turkey sandwich. It's exactly the same.

Customer: Actually, I think I'll just have a salad.

Employee: I'll be right back. [Goes in back room.] Did you hear what I just said back there?

Customer: Ummm . . . No.

Employee: Good. I mean, 'cause it wasn't about you.

Customer: Okay . . .

*Sandwich shop, Tysons Corner, Virginia*


## I'm More Interested in the *Idea* of Cheese

Customer: I would like a cheeseburger but with no cheese.

Cashier: So . . . you want a simple hamburger?

Customer: No! A cheeseburger with no cheese!

*Fast-food restaurant, New York, New York*

## So, How Far Is That from Maryland?

Woman: I want to send a money order.

Teller: Is it going out of state?

Woman: No, it's not.

Teller: Where are you sending it?

Woman: Chicago.

Teller: That's out of state.

Woman: It is?!

*Bank, Southfield, Michigan*

## Next You'll Be Claiming People Lived in Mexico Before the Spanish Colonized It!

Customer: That's a pretty name. Different.

Cashier: Yeah, you don't see it much up here. It's Mexican.

Customer: Don't you mean it's Spanish?

Cashier: No, it's Mexican in origin.

Customer: Racist.

*Sprague Avenue, Spokane, Washington*

## So You'll Have to Buy a Clue Somewhere Else

Customer on phone: Can you transfer me to the electronic section?

Clerk: Uh, anyone in particular?

Customer on phone: Yes, electronics.

Clerk: Sir, you do realize we are an electronic store, right?

*Bowie, Maryland*

## Yes, Matt Lauer Says the Same Thing

Male customer: Well, we're definitely interested. We'll be back this week to make the purchase.

Sales chick: It was a pleasure to meet you. My name is Katie.

Female customer: Oh, *Katie*. We'll remember *that* name!

Sales chick: Oh?

Female customer, whispering: Katie is the name of my other personality.

Sales chick: Oh?

Female customer, turning to male customer: Katie is not very nice, is she, darling?

Male customer: No, dear, she's not.

*Northridge, California*


## Also, Will I Meet a Tall, Dark Stranger on an Upcoming Voyage?

Customer: I need to have some work done on my car, and I want to know how much it's going to cost.

Shop guy: Okay, let's go take a look.

Customer: Well, the car isn't here, it's at my house.

Shop guy: You need to bring the car here if you want an estimate.

Customer: I don't need an estimate; I just want to know how much it's going to cost.

*Auto body shop, New Jersey*

## Lloyd Never Accepted the Constraints of the English Language

Man: Do you have the movie *Upside Down*?
Cashier: Let me check. . . . Um, no.
Man: The one about the two guys on the wine tour . . .
Cashier: You mean *Sideways*?
Man: Yeah, that one.
Cashier: It's under *S* on the wall.
Man, to friend: It's under *S*, with *Psycho*.

*Video store, Ontario, Canada*


## C'mon, I'll Drive You over to It

Employee: I can take you right to the landscaping section. Let's take the elevator here.
Customer: Boy, you really like to pamper these fat-assed people, huh? You know Texas is one of the fattest states in the nation? Don't you have stairs?
Employee: We have an escalator.

*1217 West State Highway 114, Grapevine, Texas*


## Please Hold It up So I Can See It

Customer service rep: Thank you for calling Items, Inc.* How may I help you?
Customer: I'm calling about my bill.
Customer service rep: Okay, which bill are you calling about?

Customer: The one I received.

*3445 North M-291 Highway, Independence, Missouri*

## What Early Urkel Exposure Does to Ghetto Children

Thug customer #1: Yo, man, this place is lined up!

Thug customer #2: Yo, this place got more lines than algebra class.

Thug customer #1: Man, this place prob'ly got more signs in it.

Thug customer #2: Fo' sho'. It prob'ly got more cosines in it, too.

*3090 Carling Avenue, Ottawa, Ontario, Canada*

## Then Why Are You Selling It?

Cashier: Ma'am, you do realize there's a fire ban in effect that includes charcoal grills?

Customer: Oh, I thought that was only for the locals.

*City Market, Buena Vista, Colorado*

## A Whacking Good Reason

Female customer #1: They have lotion in the women's bathroom that is phenomenal.

Female customer #2: There was a line for the women's room, so the owner let me use the men's room when nobody was in it. They didn't have any lotion in there.

Male customer: There's probably a good reason for that.

*3520 Erie Avenue, Cincinnati, Ohio*

## But on That Note, What's Your Availability?

Customer: Wow, you must be in high demand this time of year.
Employee: I guess so.
Customer: Oh, I meant the store, not you.

*Columbia, Maryland*

## Which Means I Don't Understand the Question

Mortgage rep: And, finally, may I ask you what race you are? Caucasian, African-American . . . ?
Customer: I'm Canadian.

*Fairfield, Connecticut*

## What Happens When You Use Google China

Office manager: Civil War Battlefield Protection, how can I help you?
Woman: Yes, I'm trying to find information on the Civil War and I just can't.
Office manager: Well, have you tried the Internet?
Woman: Yes, I typed "Civil War" into Google and *nothing* comes up on the Civil War.
Office manager: Really?
Woman: Yes . . . So, can you tell me who was in the Civil War?
Office manager: That would be the Northern states and the Southern states.
Woman: Not the British?
Office manager: Um, that was the Revolutionary War.

*13th & H Streets, Washington, DC*

## Error! Error! Does . . . Not . . . Compute . . . Error!

Female customer: Excuse me, what is this?

Guy behind counter: It's gazpacho soup.

Female customer: But it's cold.

Guy behind counter: It's supposed to be served chilled.

Female customer: But you said it was soup.

*Hospital cafeteria, New York, New York*

## And What About Their Screensavers? Those Are My Favorite.

Customer: Is Office 2003 the latest version of Office that's out?

Salesperson: Yeah, they most likely won't come out with a new version until Vista is released, which should be about the end of the year.

Customer: What's that?

Salesperson: Vista?

Customer: Yeah, Rista? What is that? Is that the new Office?

Salesperson: No, *Vista* is the new operating system that's coming out. Last I heard, Microsoft was planning to release it near the end of this year.

Customer: Microsoft's going to sell computers now?

Salesperson: No, Vista is the operating system that gets installed on computers. It's what makes your computer run.

Customer: Oh, yeah, I knew that already. Are you going to be carrying Microsoft's new computers?

*Willard Building, State College, Pennsylvania*

customers

## Maybe "Shape It Up" Might Have Been More Appropriate

Employee: Can I help you find something?

Female customer: No . . . Actually, yes. I can't find any CDs by Devo.

Employee: Hmmm. What genre?

Girl: I would say rock, but—

Employee: D-I-V-O?

Girl: No, D-E-V-O.

Employee: That sounds really familiar. Let me go take a look. [Begins to turn away.]

Girl: Yeah, "Whip it!" [Makes whip crack motion.]

Employee looks hurt and oblivious as he walks away.

*1515 West Highway 114, Grapevine, Texas*

## What Do You Have to Do Around Here to Get Some Freaking Champagne?!

Employee: Can I help you find something?

Customer: I'm looking for a red wine.

Employee: Cabernet, Pinot Noir, Shiraz?

Customer: No, I want a red wine.

*1017 East Main Street, Radford, Virginia*

## News Flash: Hygiene Strikeforce Raids Filthy Apartment

Irate tenant on voicemail: I came home today, and someone was in my apartment . . . *vacuuming*. . . . I feel so violated!

*3520 Lancaster Avenue, Philadelphia, Pennsylvania*

## What Are You Talking About? I'm in the Will!

Salesgirl to old lady: Well, you could use a clip or something like that to open the bracelet. . . .

Uptight lady to old lady: Or you could use a letter opener, like I do. Hmmm . . . Never mind. You'd probably stab yourself and bleed to death.

Salesgirl: Uh, yeah, that wouldn't be good. . . .

*Main Street, Rhode Island*

## When Sophisticated Taste Comes Full Circle

Irate lady: Turnips? They don't have turnips? This is why we can never leave New York.

*Gas station, Route 7, New Milford, Connecticut*

## I'd Have to Be Nuts to Do That

Lady customer: If I was going to have to get back in that line there was no way I was going to pass up the balls.

*523 North Sam Houston Parkway East, Houston, Texas*

## Her "Husband" Is Actually a Carpool-Lane Dummy

Woman: Wait, you mean to tell me there is a limit of how many of these I can have?

Pharmacy tech: Yes. You can get ten per month.

Woman: My husband is *not* going to like that. He wants more sex than that. Who only wants to have sex ten times a month?!

Pharmacy tech, looking woman up and down: Maybe it won't be the problem you think it is. . . .

*Pharmacy, Montvale, New Jersey*

## Gillette's New *Mach Seppuku*

Female shopper: Do you have ice cream?

Male worker: No, sorry. [To female worker] We *should* sell ice cream. Don't you think we should sell ice cream?

Female shopper, interrupting: Yes, you should. Where are the razors?

Male worker: For shaving?

Female shopper: No, for suicide.

*66 South Main Street, Sharon, Massachusetts*

## Except Possibly in the Upper Peninsula

Customer: I am from Wisconsin—God's country.

Insurance agent: We call Michigan God's country, too, but I don't think we have the same god.

*140 Rivers Edge Drive, Traverse City, Michigan*

## For Basil, the Long, Sun-Blinded Search Was Finally Over

Customer: Where's Sunglass Hut?
Employee: This *is* Sunglass Hut . . .

*Sydney, Australia*


## Life Are but a Dream

Eloquent customer: Our lives is a reality show.

*New Jersey*


## He's Still on Hold

Lady on cell in line: I kept waiting for him to hang up on me.
I gave him several opportunities.

*North Dakota*


## As Long as It's Not the Same Date as Halloween Again

Lady shopper #1: What day is Thanksgiving on this year?
Lady shopper #2: I don't know—Thursday or Friday?

*Springfield, Missouri*


## This Is a Singles-Only Bar

German lady tourist: Once your husband is dead you can stay.

*18th & M Streets, Washington, DC*

## And Then We'll Give Thanks

Customer on cell: Just stick the turkey baster in there and suck it all out!

*320 SW Stark Street, Portland, Oregon*

## Because Do I Ever Have the Middle East Excursion Package for You . . .

Customer: Hi.

Travel agent: Are you ready to book something today, or are you just going to ask questions?

*Queen Street, Brisbane, Australia*

## And There's Nothing I Enjoy More Than Being Taken from Behind

Man to lady lunch companion: See, the good thing about you is that you can really pack it in. I mean, most girls can't do that.

*12th & G Streets, Washington, DC*

## At Least Once a Month

Customer on cell: No, he just goes with the flow. And she is his flow.

*323 East Grand River, Howell, Michigan*

## Dude! I Was Trying to Pick Him Up.

Guard #1, checking ID: You can't come in, you're under eighteen.

Guy: What?

Guard #1: I can't let you in, you have to be eighteen.

Guy: What are you talking about? Just look at the date of my birth!

Guard #2 to the other, checking the ID: Dude, he's older than you!

Guard #1: Oh . . . Go ahead, then.

*Tel Aviv, Israel*


## In the Jar on My Nightstand Where They Always Are. Why?

Shopper chick #1: He is the best. He called me yesterday and said that he really needed me and that he almost cried about how much he misses me—

Shopper chick #2: Where's his balls?!

*Stockholm, Sweden*


## Her Dentist Is Psyched!

Bimbette #1: I get really intimate with people that stick things in my mouth.

Bimbette #2: Isn't it always like that?

*Mannheim, Germany*

## Although You Do Want Her to Be Smart Enough to Pull Her Pants Down

Bar patron #1: I couldn't be with her—she's so stupid.

Bar patron #2: She doesn't have to be smart to pull her pants down. You don't want her to pass the Bar Exam for you, you want her to give up the pussy.

Bar patron #1: Good point.

*South Illinois Street, Indianapolis, Indiana*


## And Even Then, I Make You Eat Only Organic Foods for Two Days Beforehand

Tipsy chick #1: So, what about the new guy?

Tipsy chick #2: James*? He doodled on me! I mean, we have to be dating for at least a few weeks before you get to doodle on me.

*Bar, 254 Crown Street, New Haven, Connecticut*


## It's the Ghosts of a Thousand Drunken Derelicts!

Teen boy: Dude, the haunted house pees on you!

*Superstition Springs Mall, Mesa, Arizona*


## Without the Passive Resistance

Young male shopper: I do what I can.

Young lady shopper: You are like a big, hairy Gandhi.

*Austin, Texas*

## Or Trying Very Hard to Get in Your Daughter's Pants

Mom: I don't like your bag.

Daughter: I bought it when I went shopping with Alex.*

Mom: That's the problem—you should never take a guy shopping with you.

Daughter: But I go shopping with Aaron* all of the time. I bought those shoes you like with him.

Mom: That's different. He's gay.

*Clothing store, 5808 South 144th Street, Omaha, Nebraska*

# ((outside the cubicle

## Kindly Do Not Demonstrate

Lady peon: . . . So if you've never done it before, it's going to hurt the first time and maybe even bleed a bit.

Male peon: Uh-huh.

Lady peon: So don't be afraid. You should try it. It's definitely worth it.

Other people in elevator shuffle uncomfortably.

Lady peon: Um . . . So, flossing is crucial to good dental hygiene. . . .

*Houston, Texas*

## For Your Comfort and Safety, Remember That Kids Are Pretty Literal

School social worker to kindergartner on lap: So, what happened right before you ran out of your classroom?

Kindergartner: I'm peeing.

Social worker: What do you mean, you're peeing?

Kindergartner: I'm peeing.

Social worker: [Jumps up, displaying huge wet spot on her pants.]

Kindergartner: I *told* you I was peeing.

*5130 Roxbury Road, Indianapolis, Indiana*

## Didn't I Tell You? I'm Guilty.

Defense attorney: I'm going back to the office. God, I hate days like this. Losing blows.

Defendant: Hey, sorry, man. But really, you didn't have a chance.

*300 East Bay Street, Jacksonville, Florida*

## Tonight on WWE *SmackDown*: Clash of the Bureaucrats!

FBI agent: Excuse me, I'm an investigator for the FBI. I would like a copy of a student's transcript.

Registrar: Okay, you need to pay a seven-dollar transcript fee.

FBI agent: Uh, I don't think I need to pay that. I'm an investigator for the FBI.

Registrar: *Everybody* has to pay for a transcript.

FBI agent: I think I will have to speak to your supervisor.

Registrar: I'm sorry, but that's what the sign says.

*John Jay College of Criminal Justice, 10th Avenue, New York, New York*

## Rain Man: Hey!

Angry cop: Fucking college kids make me sick. It's disgusting. You're the smartest, most retarded people in the world!

*Easton Avenue, New Brunswick, New Jersey*

## Marx Predicted This

Little girl to employee making a purchase: You can't shop here! You're supposed to work! You're not people!

*801 North Congress Avenue, Boynton Beach, Florida*

outside the cubicle

## In Death Everyone Gets a Little Classier

Lawyer: So, you were locked in a room that had a gas leak?

Client: Yeah. Man, we was trying to get out quick as we could. I mean, if we didn't make it out when we did, we could've been sophisticated!

Lawyer: Asphyxiated?

Client: Whatever.

*Public Square, Cleveland, Ohio*

## There Are No Stupid Questions. Oh, Wait . . .

Interviewer: Just fill out this application and wait to be called for the interview.

Interviewee: Does it matter if I got a crack possession against me?

*420 Harding Road, Nashville, Tennessee*

## He Has Those Shifty Eyes

Teacher: *Uncertain.* What does *uncertain* mean?

Seven-year-old boy: Like, you're not sure about it?

Teacher: Good! What's an example of something you're un-certain about?

Seven-year-old boy, after thinking for a moment: God.

*1554 Sepulveda Boulevard, Los Angeles, California*

## Aren't Asians Supposed to Be Smart?

Interviewer: Have you ever had to deal with rude or irate clients over the telephone?

Asian interviewee: Yes, at my last job I had to call the USA, and you know how rude they can be. . . .

Interviewer: Yes, I know all too well considering I am American and so is this company. This interview is now finished. Try not to hit my car on your way out of the parking lot. . . . You know how Asians can't drive.

*Toronto, Ontario, Canada*

## Little Nipper Plans to Tuck

Mom: Tell your aunt what you want to be when you grow up.

Two-year-old son: A plastic surgeon!

Mom: And why is that?

Two-year-old son: Because Mommy needs work!

*Café, Hurst, Texas*

## If It's Too Hard to Process, Just Pretend You Didn't Hear It

Avis clerk: I just love your little beanie!

Jewish guy: It's actually called a yarmulke. I'm Jewish, and all Jewish men wear them.

Avis clerk: Oh! Well, you have yourself a merry Christmas!

*Charlotte Douglas International Airport, Charlotte, North Carolina*

## Are You Sure You Don't Mean *Joseph* Smith?

Voice over loudspeaker: John Smith, please report to baggage claim to meet your wife and girlfriend. John Smith to baggage claim, meet your wife and girlfriend.

*Oakland International Airport, Oakland, California*

## Not Why I Went to Law School, but What Are Ya Gonna Do?

Criminal defense attorney: Leave me alone. I have to get back to work.
Peon: Why is that?
Criminal defense attorney: I have a client that might actually be innocent.

*39 South LaSalle Street, Chicago, Illinois*

## News Flash: Student Expelled for Refusing to "Dumb Down" Answers

Teacher: Scott,* can you give the next answer?
Student: Religion is the belief in a supernatural and the relationship with this being.
Teacher: Could you please speak normally next time?
Student: I am.

*High school, Whitby, Ontario, Canada*

## He's Adopted

Patient: Yeah, I have a twin brother about my age.

*Hospital, New York, New York*

## He's Manager for a Reason

Restaurant manager to homeless man panhandling inside the restaurant: You need to leave right now.

Homeless man: Man, how you know I not here for some crab cakes and fine wine?

Restaurant manager: Because you have human shit all over your pants.

*Illinois Street, Indianapolis, Indiana*

## And Blackmail? That Pretty Legal, Also?

Lawyer: Put your John Hancock on these documents, please.

Daughter: You sure this is legal? I mean, with me being your kid and all?

Lawyer: It is very legal. Far more legal than any of the drugs you have experimented with on my credit card.

*Broad Street, Louisville, Georgia*

## He Aced the Mixed Drinks Portion of the Bar Exam

Defense attorney: Objection, Your Honor. The prosecution continues to assert this witness is an expert but has offered no evidence to support the claim.

Judge: Sustained. Mr. Martin,* is this witness your expert?

Prosecutor: Yes, Your Honor.

Judge: Would you care to establish for the court why the witness is an expert in the field of pediatrics?

Prosecutor: 'Cause he . . . ummm . . . knows stuff?

*State Court, Austin, Texas*

## It's Actually a Clever Piece of Performance Art Commenting on the Injustice of the Electric Chair as a Means of Execution

Cop: Put the knife down—you don't want to do this.

Depressed guy: *Stay back!* I'm serious, I'll do it!

Cop: Come on, put the knife down so we can talk.

Depressed guy: *Stay back!*

Cop, pulling out his Taser: Okay, last chance—put the knife down or I'll Tase you!

Depressed guy: Stop, I don't want to get hurt!

*Cromwell, Connecticut*

## The Resident's Box Has Always Been Public

Resident: Patient was seen today at his home. He's still complaining that the beams from Oregon are bothering him, but he said they aren't affecting him too badly right now. In fact, he said that they don't affect men too much in general—it's really women who should be worried about the beams. Especially, he said, when they're aimed at women's private boxes.

Social worker: Did you just say "private boxes"?

*Psychiatric clinic, Tulsa, Oklahoma*

## His Sensitivity Might Be Better Appreciated at Country Curtains

Guy to wife: Hey, look at this guy's picture on the wall. He looks like he's miserable and doesn't like being at work.

Employee whose picture is on the wall: That was taken on a bad hair day!

Man: Oh . . . sorry. Where would you find paint?

*Home-repair store, Dallas, Texas*


## An Employee You Can Almost Count On

Interviewer: So, how would you say you handle changes in the workplace?

Interviewee: Um . . . Oh! I'm really good with change. I used to work a cash register, and if the total came to $7.49 and they gave me a ten, I'd give them three . . . no . . . $2.60 . . . uh . . . $2.51!

Interviewer: Uh . . . okay!

*Ames, Iowa*


## I Clung to the Ceiling Until the Board of Regents Granted Me Tenure

Japanese professor: The peroxides are very volatile. If you drop them we have to be out of the building before they hit the floor.

Grad student: I won't drop them.

Japanese professor: And only Japanese ninjas can move that fast.

outside the cubicle

177

Grad student: Okay.
Japanese professor: I am well-trained in the art of the ninja.

*10900 Euclid Avenue, Cleveland, Ohio*

## And It Took *Him* Three Days to Get over It

First-grade teacher: *Jacob!* Give me those! Those are *nails*!
   Nails are unsafe and do not belong in your hands!
Student: Pshhh, unless you're *Jesus*!

*New York, New York*

## She Unwittingly Picked Her Career on Opposite Day

Very pregnant elementary school teacher: God, I *hate*
   screaming kids!

*1 Raider Circle, Houston, Texas*

## What Jesus Would Have Done

Male worker: Was this in DC?
Lady worker: No! It was in Maryland, where I live! Right be-
   hind my condo building! I was so upset!
Male worker: Huh.
Lady worker: If I had a gun, I tell you what—I would have
   shot him as he was running away. I was so upset. The lit-
   tle bitch would have been dead. [She exits the elevator.]
   Have a blessed day!

*5600 Fishers Lane, Rockville, Maryland*

## His Next Call Is to Napa Auto Parts to Make Dinner Reservations

Hostess: Thank you for calling Napa Twenty-nine, how can I help you? . . . I'm sorry, sir, this is a restaurant, not an auto parts store. . . . No, sir, this is not Napa Auto Parts. . . . No, sir. . . . Sir, this is a restaurant. I don't know how much a carburetor costs. . . . Sir, I really don't. . . . Three hundred dollars and eighty-nine cents. . . . Yes, sir. Have a nice evening.

*280 Teller Street, Corona, California*


## I'm Gonna Say, "Courtney Love," but That's Just a Shot in the Dark

Girl caller: Hi, I want to report a woman lying facedown in the road.
Police receptionist: What does she look like?

*Rosemead, California*


## In Fact, That's the Dictionary Definition of "Okay"

Voice over PA: If you see people in camouflage running around with guns and hear explosions, it is okay.

*Hall Drive, Wilmington, Delaware*


## But I'm Watching You, Pal

Security guard: Um, we have a problem here.
Traveler: And what might that be?

Security guard: Do you have any other form of identification? Your driver's license is expired.

Traveler: No, it's not . . . This is 2006.

Security guard: You may pass.

*General Mitchell Airport, Milwaukee, Wisconsin*

## Another Victim of the "Math Is Hard" Barbie

Barista: What are *you* going to do when you grow up?

Little girl: Doctor.

Barista: You want to be a doctor? That's wonderful!

Little girl: No. Mommy told me to marry a doctor and have kids. I want twenty-seven!

*Fort Valley Road, Flagstaff, Arizona*

## Either Way, Really

Plumber: What do I have to do to install gas lines?

Admin: You have to take our class and enroll in a drug and alcohol testing program.

Plumber: You mean I gotta be on drugs to install gas lines?

Admin: No, sir, you have to *not* be on drugs.

Plumber: Oh, okay. I can do that.

*5461 Southwyck Boulevard, Toledo, Ohio*

## No, That's Question #15

Nurse pointing to birth control questionnaire: Ma'am, I think you answered this question incorrectly.

Fifteen-year-old girl: No, that's right.

Nurse: It asks how long you've been with your current partner. You said, "Five minutes."

Fifteen-year-old girl: That's how long it took.

*616 Court Street, Los Angeles, California*

## Cuban Business Customs: The Short Course

Canadian: Is there anything I should know about Cuban business customs before we get started?

Translator: No.

Girl with tray of espressos walks in and hands one to each person.

Canadian: I don't drink coffee.

Translator: You do today.

*Cuban Health Ministry, Havana, Cuba*

## And I Read a Lot of Nietzsche

Interviewer: What would you say your strengths are?

Buff interviewee: Arms and back.

*Dresden Nuclear Power Plant, Morris, Illinois*

## Tupac's Propaganda Machine, on the Other Hand, Is Alive and Thriving

Counselor: Is that a Tupac T-shirt? You're five. Tupac wasn't alive when you were born. What do you know about Tupac?

Kid: I know the haters killed him.

Counselor: Touché.

*Richmond, Virginia*

## He Was Much Worse Before the Diversity Training

Suit: You're Asian, so I bet you want tea. We Americans like our morning coffee.

Asian interviewee #1: No, I had Starbucks on the way here.

Suit: We Americans like milk in our coffee. Asians drink it black, right?

Asian interviewee #2: No, I take mine light and sweet.

Suit: Well, you still wanna work here, right?

*Midtown, New York, New York*

## From the Shaolin Preschool Songbook

Coworker: If you're happy and you know it . . .

Two-year-old daughter: . . . Don't touch a knife!

*1065 Williams Street, Atlanta, Georgia*

## So I Got This *L* Tattooed on My Forehead

Guy: So, it turned out my phone wasn't broken. It was just nobody wanted to call me.

*Filton Road, Bristol, England*

## What Happens When Spell-Check Infiltrates Speech

Trainee: So, can you tell me why your mother can't walk?
Girl: Her leg was amputated, and she can't walk on her prostate.

*Home office, Santa Barbara, California*


## Cheap Dinner Dates?

Loud secretary: What do you call people who are from Dutch?

*Princeton, New Jersey*


## No, He's *Reading* Too Loud

Children's librarian: Do you mind?
Chick with breast exposed, nursing her baby: I'm sorry, is he sucking too loud?

*Library, Rock Hill, South Carolina*


## Jack Spratt for the Twenty-First Century

Intern: I've never had butt sex. I'm saving it for marriage. Since I'm not a virgin anymore, I have to save something for my husband.
Friend: You're so dumb. You should have done what I did. I *only* have butt sex, so I'm still a virgin.

*The Pour House Bar, Capitol Hill, Washington, DC*

outside the cubicle

## She's Already Seen His Briefs

Lawyer: Hey, here's something that might interest you!
Secretary: I doubt it.

*3415 South Sepulveda Boulevard, Los Angeles, California*

## Mainstreaming Dung-Beetle-Americans in the Public Schools May Have Been a Mistake

Teacher #1: I can't teach this kid anymore.
Teacher #2: Why?
Teacher #1: He can't keep his hands out of his pants.
Teacher #2: So?
Teacher #1: Look, do I have to spell it out? He doesn't know the difference between shit and food.
Teacher #2: Oh my god, I'm gonna barf.
Teacher #1: Not around this kid. He might think it's a snack.

*3035 Desert Marigold Lane, Las Vegas, Nevada*

## Needless to Say, the White One Is Whole Foods

Classmate #1: I'm gonna shave your head and sell your hair on the black market!
Classmate #2: Why would black people want his hair?
Classmate #3, after laughter subsides: Where is the black market, anyway?

*High school, Mount Vernon, Texas*

## It Was an Attempted Coop d'État

Girl #1: There was a ruckus in the office, but we sorted it out.

Girl #2: It's funny—whenever I think of the word *ruckus* I think of, like, chickens.

Girl #3: Oh my god, there were chickens in the office?

*University Drive, Gold Coast, Australia*

## She Faked That One

Secretary: Put it in! Put it in! Faster, c'mon! I can't take it! Put it in! [Giggles.]

Worker: Ready? Here we go. [Excessive grunting.]

Secretary: Oh, yeah, that feels great! Oh, *yes*.

Boss walks by, looking in office: What the hell is going on here?

Secretary: He just put the air conditioner in!

*2000 Peel Street, Montreal, Quebec, Canada*

## All Hell Broke Loose When She Caught Him Reading the Jolly Rancher Label

Mom to young child: That's just more junk. I'm not going to buy you something to write with. How 'bout I get you some candy instead?

*Dollar Store, Detroit, Michigan*

## He Gets Smarter When He Drinks

Frat boy: Gimme something like a whiskey sour, but don't put
    Jack Daniel's or anything like that in it. I don't like whiskey!
Bartender: Well, what do you want in it instead of whiskey?
Frat boy: Use Jim Beam—I fucking love Jim Beam!

*Evolution Nightclub, Athens, Ohio*

## So Anyway, Whatever Problem You're Having Is *Your* Fault. Questions?

Techie answering phone: Hello, this is Brenda.* . . . No, I
    wasn't just speaking to someone on the phone. . . . I'm
    positive! I work in IT, so I rarely talk to anyone.

*100 Sylvan Road, Woburn, Massachusetts*

## The Best Diagnosis Canada's Health Services Have Been Able to Come up With

Student #1: Do you have a learning disability or something?
Student #2: Yeah, I'm ADD.
Student #1: Oh.
Student #2: Just kidding! I'm just stupid.

*Saskatoon, Saskatchewan, Canada*

## Because I've Heard Stories About These "Dingoes"

Employee on phone with child care center: Ummm, I don't
    know . . . Do you have trouble with children escaping?

*Canberra, Australia*

## Monica Lewinsky: Worked for Me!

Interview consultant: Always be aware of what you are saying during an interview. I have seen interviews fall apart over a single word.

Student: Like what word?

Interview consultant: The word was *fuck*.

*Washington College of Law, 4801 Massachusetts Avenue NW, Washington, DC*


## Tell You What—Half Price for You. You Can Give the Six Dollars to Me.

Girl #1: Ummm, we need to make copies, and we don't want to spend a lot of money.

Student worker: The copier over there is ten cents, same as everywhere on campus.

Girl #1: That's so expensive!

Student worker: You could also scan the papers and print them out. That's free.

Girl #1: What do you mean?

Student worker: Ummm, you can put them on the scanner, hit Scan, and then when they pop up, hit Print.

Girl #1: I don't know about this whole scanning thing—it sounds really complicated.

Girl #2: But that sounds better than making copies. I mean, we only need twelve, and I don't want to spend twelve dollars.

*Campus library, Bemidji State University, Bemidji, Minnesota*

outside the cubicle

## Why Kiwi Teachers Smell

Teacher #1: I think I should just become a hooker.
Teacher #2: Yeah, but think of the all the washing you would have to do.

*New Zealand*

## Lifting, Puking, and Shooting: The Lloyd Roid Story

Designer: I can't find a photo to represent personal trainers. The only stock images we have are too creepy—look kind of like an after-school special.

Writer: Like a molesting-kids after-school special? Or the kind about bulimia?

Designer: A cross between those and the ones about steroids.

Creative director: Oh, that sounds okay. Use whatever you guys have.

*16340 North Scottsdale Road, Scottsdale, Arizona*

## Well, I Do Have a Master's in Evacuation

Attorney: Are you qualified to give a urine sample?

*355 North Euclid Avenue, Tucson, Arizona*

## Even a Dumb Chick Is Right Once Every Thousand Years

Bimbette clerk #1: Like, what's a millennium?

Bimbette clerk #2: I think it's, like, when the year changes or something.

*Video store, Calgary, Alberta, Canada*

## Any Excuse to Tell That Story

Nurse: She's been so much better today. Chatty. She still walks around like this [puts chin to chest], but she came up to me and was like, "How are you today?" I said, "Huh? Oh, I'm fine!" Maybe it's the Celexa.

Psychiatrist: Actually, we're weaning her off the Celexa. We started her on Effexor.

Nurse: Oh, well, maybe that's it.

Psychiatrist: She's only been on it one day. That wouldn't really be long enough.

Nurse: No, that's not . . . Celexa . . . I think I was taking that when I got into a fight at the airport. You know those guys with the M16s? Well, I told this one bitch I was gonna jump over the counter and take her out.

Psychiatrist: That was Celexa?

Nurse, smiling: Yeah.

*Hospital, Salem, Oregon*

## Yeah, They Have All Kinds of Crap

Female suit: This chair is too high. My feet barely touch the floor. I should order a step stool from the office supplies department. Do you have the catalog?

Male suit: They have stool samples in there?

*2nd Street, Jersey City, New Jersey*

outside the cubicle

## She Couldn't Find the Container of White Powder

Blonde barmaid: What's in a whiskey and Coke?

*Pesto Café, Fayetteville, Arkansas*

## One Way to Find Out

Control room guy: I'm sorry, but if you get a hard-on from another guy, *you're gay*. You can't just say you were just acting. DeNiro couldn't even act that well.

*Toronto, Ontario, Canada*

## She's Adopted, So It Isn't His Fault

Suit: I'm looking for my daughter. She was going to meet us at McDonald's, but it's closed so I need to tell her.
Clerk: Oh, is she a very pretty girl?
Suit: Not really.
Clerk: Oh.

*1535 Bacharach Boulevard, Atlantic City, New Jersey*

## Next You'll Be Reading Our Subpoenas and Overdue Bills

Young boy: Mom! We've been in line for a really long time!
Mom: No, not really. Stop complaining.
Young boy: Yes we have! We got here at ten, and it's almost twelve thirty!
Mom: Damn the public school system for teaching you how to tell time.

*PETCO, Enfield, Connecticut*

## Wait, No! That's What the Frogs *Want*!

Pilot: Tower, there's a piece of foreign object debris on the taxiway in front of the tower.
Tower: Roger, we'll send a truck right out to pick it up.
Pilot: Tower, disregard the FOD. It just hopped off the taxiway.
Tower: Disregarding.

*Air Force pilot training base, Texas*

## Remember? Those Nine Planes?

Delivery driver: I've never had to stop and check in before.
Guard: Yes, you have. We started doin' it after two-eleven.
Delivery driver: You mean nine-eleven?
Guard, rolling eyes: No. Two-eleven, when them people crashed them planes. Two-eleven.
Delivery driver: That was in September.
Guard: *Two-eleven*.

*Circle Center Mall Security Office, Indianapolis, Indiana*

## So, Pizza or Chinese?

Consultant: This meeting is just too important to involve company employees.

*100 East Rivercenter Boulevard, Covington, Kentucky*

## And She Was So Smart for Figuring That Out

Female clerk: Did you notice the way their baby looked?
Guy: Um, yeah.

Female clerk: It's because she didn't do drugs or alcohol when she was pregnant. It makes a big difference, you know? That's why the baby is so smart.

*Tulsa, Oklahoma*


## See the Gauloises, the Berets, and the Spacecraft?

Little girl pointing to *Coneheads*: Daddy, what's wrong with those people?

Dad: Oh, they're just from France.

*Blockbuster, University Village, Seattle, Washington*


## I'm Considering Bumping It Up to "Ti-Mika" If I Make Partner

Girl #1: Yeah, and that's why I changed my name.

Girl #2: For real? What was it before?

Girl #1: I changed it from Te-mika to Ta-mika. Sounds more professional.

Girl #2: Oooh, girl, you know you right.

*1300 19th Street, Washington, DC*


## Goering Was Especially Tasty

Male worker: We're gonna make some bratwurst.

Lady worker #1: What's the difference between sausage and bratwurst?

Lady worker #2: Well, bratwurst is German.

Lady worker #1: So they're just German pigs?

*Company picnic, Montclair, New Jersey*

## You Can't Let People Get Away with Basing Their Lives on Eighties Movies

Security guard: I walked in on him making love to a mannequin, so I kicked the shit out of him.

*Hazeldean Mall, Kanata, Ontario, Canada*


## The Team That Smells Together Jells Together?

Senior research analyst: Someone's all cologned up in here.
Team leader: I think most of us are. We're a good-smelling team.

*Elevator, 4833 Rugby Avenue, Bethesda, Maryland*


## After Successfully Outlawing Science, Kansas Gets Right to Work on Math

City council member: I thought we just voted that down unanimously with the exception of one or two votes.

*Capitol grounds, Topeka, Kansas*


## You Dope. What Are the Odds It Could Be Anybody Else?

Suit on cell: Hey, man, what's going on? . . . So, I heard that two cops shot a dude, and I was just wondering if it was you.

*44th Street & Broadway, New York, New York*

## Made from 100 Percent USDA Grade A Cops

Temp: All the food here is good—especially the bacon. I mean, this is real bacon, not the kind you buy at the store.

*Culinary school, Pasadena, California*

## I Love the Law: The Smell of the Jury, the Sobbing of the Witness . . .

Lawyer #1: So, I finally got myself in front of a jury!
Lawyer #2: Really?
Lawyer #1: Yeah! It was a rape case.
Lawyer #2: That's fantastic! Well, for you, anyway.

*Allegan Street, Lansing, Michigan*

## If I'm Ever Too Old to Chuckle at the Phrase "Do It," Pull the Plug

Man: It's okay. We can still do it in my office.
Woman: That sounds fantastic.

*Route 9, Wellesley Hills, Massachusetts*

## At Last We Learn How *Howard the Duck* Got Greenlighted

Writer: I told you that duck was evil.
Designer: I know.
Writer: But you kept trying to squeeze him in the layout anyway.

Designer: I know. He looked so tempting when I first saw him, but that duck was the spawn of Satan.

Writer: I told you he was a freak.

Designer: He lured me in!

*16340 North Scottsdale Road, Scottsdale, Arizona*

## It's Their Wellness Program

General manager: Feeling better today?

Waitress, laughing: Oh, yes!

General manager: Why are you laughing?

Waitress: Oh, it's nothing.

General manager: No, tell me!

Waitress: I can't!

General manager: Is it girl stuff?

Waitress: No.

General manager: Well, then tell me!

Waitress: Okay. I'm feeling better because I got really fucking stoned last night.

General manager: Dopehead.

*Beaumont, Texas*

## Snakes in a Colon

Suit #1: So, she said the snake got loose in her apartment, and they can't find it.

Suit #2: Well, until they do she's gonna have to sleep with her ass up against the wall!

*32nd Street, Jersey City, New Jersey*

## In the Same Way That Humans Are Made of "Long Pig"

Dad: What are birds made of?

Little girl: Chicken?

*505 Broadway, Scottsbluff, Nebraska*

## I Nodded Off During the Part About the Rain Forests

Drama teacher: We're going to McDonald's. Did you want us to pick something up for you?

Hippie guitar teacher: No, I don't eat there.

Drama teacher: Why, because of the movie *Super Size Me*?

Hippie guitar teacher: No, I stopped eating there ever since they started cutting down the rain forests to make room for more cow pastures for their meat.

Drama teacher: So . . . then . . . you *don't* want McDonald's?

*1311 East Katella Avenue, Orange, California*

## So That's Why People Go into Hairstyling

Stylist on phone: Oh, I gave you the wrong phone number. . . . So, is that, like, a fact-smile? A fact-smile. It says here the fact-smile number is 555-9513.*

*South Loop, Chicago, Illinois*

## Luckily the Doublemint Twins Were There to Handle Any Gum Questions That Might Have Arisen

Man: So, what's that building over there?
Tour guide: That's the Wrigley Building.
Man: What does Wrigley do?
Tour guide: They make gum.
Man: Gum? Really? What kind of gum?

*Michigan Avenue, Chicago, Illinois*

## She Doesn't Like Doing Either, She Just Likes Talking About Them

Nerd #1: All Kelly* talks about is food and sex.
Nerd #2: Yeah, what do you think she likes doing more—talking about eating while having sex, or talking about fucking while having lunch?

*333 Pfingsten Road, Northbrook, Illinois*

## Especially the Cats' Eyes

Kindergarten boy: Mrs. Jones,* I need to go to the bathroom.
Mrs. Jones: No, you just went.
Kindergarten boy: Please, Mrs. Jones, I gotta go.
Mrs. Jones: No, you were told you had to wait.
Kindergarten boy: But I have to go now! My marbles are itchy!

*Manitoba, Canada*

## I, on the Other Hand, Will Be Seeing It for the First Time

Mortgage guy: I've lost twelve pounds over the last two weeks!

Realtor chick: I'm gonna miss your chubby.

*Yorba Linda, California*


## Miss Anna Phylactic's Shocking Lunch

Young lady: Are there nuts in the apple walnut salad?

Dining companion, sarcastically: No, it's a new type of apple.

Young lady: Good, because I'm allergic to nuts, and I really want that salad.

Waiter: Do you want the half salad or the whole?

*858 Tittabawassee Road, Saginaw, Michigan*


## Close . . . It's Actually Global *Luke*warming

Professor: You will have those students that don't show up to class or office hours or that don't care about their grades. . . . What causes this?

Teacher's assistant: Global warming?

*University of Texas, Austin, Texas*

## Either a Seventy-Five-Gallon Mixer or That Red-and-White Twine They Tie Cakes Up With

Elderly woman to husband: I told you we wouldn't find it here! I told you the only place we'd find it was a hardware store or a bakery!

*Department store, Glendale, Arizona*


## A Better Solution Than "Always Turn Left"

Receptionist on phone: I know, this piercing is the best! Now whenever I have sex with someone really stupid, they are bound to find it!

*London, England*


## Guy Laroche, Guy de Maupassant . . .

Local public radio reporter: Nurse Smith* is responsible for the health of over two thousand students in the school district, but she seems to know many of them individually and calls them by name as she passes them in the hallway. . . .
School nurse, to kids: Hey, guys.

*Chapel Hill, North Carolina*


## Probably Wouldn't Share Her Toothbrush, Either

Bar skank: And she got all pissy at me because I wouldn't share my sex toys with her.

*1760 Camino Del Río North, San Diego, California*

## Actually, That's Just the Easy-Bake Oven I Tuck to Comfort Me in Times Like These

Woman: I'm getting so fat.

Attorney hubby: You're not fat.

Woman: Aw, well—

Attorney hubby: You're old. You just *look* fat.

*319 West Woodlawn Avenue, Louisville, Kentucky*

## You Could Probably Steal One from a White Castle in the Bronx and No One Would Notice for a Week

Lady suit: Oh, I want the baby, I just don't want the pregnancy. If I could just go to a fast-food place and order a baby, I would.

*4910 16th Street, Indianapolis, Indiana*

## Michael Douglas Reprises His "Greed Is Good" Speech from *Wall Street*

Broker on phone: Blame it on greed. . . . Uh-huh . . . No, I'm saying that greed is a well-known, widely accepted motivator, so just say it was greed. They'll understand.

*10960 Wilshire Boulevard, Los Angeles, California*

## I Will Now Return to My Reverie Already in Progress

Lawyer on phone: Y'know, I wasn't really paying attention to what you were saying, but I am leaning towards agreeing with you.

*St. Petersburg, Florida*


## But When It Comes to Self-Abuse, Nothing Tops Alcohol and Baccarat

Grandma to stranger: Meth is way worse than heroin.
Granddaughter: What?
Grandma: Oh. Um, nothing, honey . . . Never mind. Aren't we here to gamble and drink?

*Caesars Indiana Hotel and Casino, Elizabeth, Indiana*


## This, for Example, Appears to Be a Videotape from the Reagan Years

New mother peon: You would not believe all the stuff that keeps coming out of your body.

*375 Hudson Street, New York, New York*


## Epitaph: "Six Feet, Seven Inches"

Volunteer teen #1: How far do you think this sweat drop will fly if I smack it with a hammer?
Volunteer teen #2: Hey, yeah, like *CSI*! Your forehead is real sweaty—smack it first.

*Habitat for Humanity build site, Mississippi Gulf Coast*

## In the UN Intramural League, We're Just "Dem Bums"

Engineer to lunchroom: So, do you guys know if we're officially called "United States of America," or is it just
"United States"?

*413 Pine Street, Seattle, Washington*

## Some of That Is Just Normal Post-Culinary Sadness

Engineer #1: Drew,* you're having corned beef again?
Team leader: Yeah, I got a big piece of it and cooked it all at
once.
Engineer #2: Did you get it at Costco? It's real cheap there.
Team leader: Yeah, but the thing that sucks is it shrinks
when you put it in the oven. You're thinking you have a
big piece of meat, and then you pull it out and you're all
disappointed.

*Deer Park, Illinois*

## Never Lose Bets to Your Children

Parent to teacher: Would it be possible for students to have
extra recess time instead of silent reading?

*Pittsburgh, Pennsylvania*

## You Know That Rumor That Iron Filings Are Better Than Cocaine?

Suit on cell: What made you stick a magnet up your nose?

*5th & Jackson Streets, Topeka, Kansas*


## Still Curious about the Gasoline, George?

Computer nerd: Last night I had to set my monkey on fire.

*California State University, Northridge, California*


## Nope, Just Thought You Might Need Help Getting That Desk onto Your Truck

Assistant: Are you stealing things already?
Marketing rep: Are you saying that because I'm black?

*9401 West Brown Deer Road, Milwaukee, Wisconsin*


## I'm So Glad I Still Live with My Mother

Receptionist: I thought she was going to tell me I was fat, but *nooo*—she just wanted to tell me that I smell bad.

*Andover Park West, Tukwila, Washington*


## That Explains Some of the Stains, Though

Lawyer: Oh, he's a philanderer?
Legal assistant: No, he works at a paint store.

*14340 57th Avenue, Surrey, British Columbia, Canada*

## A Deal They Were Willing to Swallow

Salesman: They like us. We leave a good taste in their mouth.

*Bay Street, Toronto, Ontario, Canada*

## Your Daughter Is So Precocious!

Little girl pointing to ad poster: Dog!
Father: No, honey, that's Ellen DeGeneres.

*Target shopping center, Avon, Indiana*

## The Violence Is Good, but I Always End Up Married to Some Vietnamese Girl

Male interviewer: So, where are you from?
Female applicant: I'm from here, but all my family is from Vietnam.
Male interviewer: Yeah? My ex-wife is from Vietnam. Ever since that war over there, I haven't really been a fan of wars, y'know?

*Doc Green's, Cumberland Boulevard, Atlanta, Georgia*

## How Do You Think I Got This Job?

Producer on phone: I don't know how to make this more clear: *Eat the bugs! You have to eat the bugs!* Open your mouth, plug your nose, *and shove the bugs in your mouth!*

*6727 Odessa Avenue, Van Nuys, California*

## I'll Eat What I Can and Take the Rest Home for Breakfast

Suit on cell: Yeah, so I'll just eat a light dinner and when we get there we can share a cowboy.... Oh, yeah, that sounds much better!

*Tucson, Arizona*

## In This Month's *New England Journal of Medicine*: "Insurance Forms and the Placebo Effect"

Doctor #1: So, I called him when he didn't show up for his visit and told him I was waiting for him. He told me that he came, signed in, filled out the insurance paperwork, answered some questions, then left and went home.

Doctor #2: What an idiot. Don't people realize that when you have a doctor's appointment you're actually supposed to go in to see the doctor?

*Boston, Massachusetts*

## Somebody Hit His "Reset" Button

Customer service rep: Do you know your son's name? Your secret question is, "What is your son's name?" Do you know your son's name?

Person resetting password: No, ma'am, I don't know what that is, either.

*Mishawka, Indiana*

### And of Course He Was There at the Time

Bimbette clerk: She really didn't betray him other than sleeping with someone else.

*1300 Riverside Avenue, Fort Collins, Colorado*

### The Internet Has Somewhat Dampened Joshua's Sense of Wonder

Office peon: What I really wanna see is a baby shot out of a cannon through a waterfall of gasoline, over a bundle of lit sparklers, and knock an old lady off a horse, 'cause then I could say I really saw something.

*Dearborn, Michigan*

### I Said, "Mr. Samsa, There's Nothing You Can Do!"

Border patrol agent: I tried to tell the guy his brother was dead. Metamorphosis had already set in.

*3423 Interstate Highway 35, Cotulla, Texas*

### And I Can Start Drinking Overtime

Man buying lottery ticket in liquor store: If I win this, the old lady can cut back to part-time.

*725 West Golf Road, Hoffman Estates, Illinois*

### One That Can Be Cured by Exorcise

Sorority girl: "Diabolico . . ." That means he's diabetic, right?

Classmate: No, it means diabolic.

Sorority girl: So, diabolic . . . Is that, like, a medical condition?

*Spanish class, University of Arizona, Tucson, Arizona*

## But That Wasn't Working, So I Switched to George

Suit #1: So, I was banging Erica* in her office, and she started crying. It reminded me of George and Meredith in *Grey's Anatomy.*

Suit #2: Wow! That must have been a turnoff.

Suit #1: No, I kept going. I just pretended I was banging Meredith.

*80 J Street, Sacramento, California*

## Until OSHA Designates You a Superfund Site

Employee to fiancé who just arrived to pick her up: I feel so dirty right now. . . . And not the good kind of dirty. . . .

Fiancé: I'll take what I can get!

*1065 Williams Street, Atlanta, Georgia*

## Oh, Free Cake? Count Me In.

Lady suit on cell: I don't see why I should have to buy her a present just because the condom broke.

*1750 Connecticut Avenue, Washington, DC*

## Different Colors, at Least! Geez!

Lady clerk on cell: You don't buy your fiancée and your friend the same dildo for Christmas. . . . Especially not when we know each other and talk to each other! Maybe I won't marry you. . . .

*Asheville Mall, Asheville, North Carolina*

## And Another Thing—Who Are You Callin' "Gross"?

Truck driver: Lemme tell you somethin'—I didn't pay for no net. I didn't want no net! And my check said I paid for a *net*?! [Receptionist explains net pay.] All I know is I didn't ask for a net! [Hangs up.]

*Trucking office, North Carolina*

## If Only I Had a Crate to Fill My Barrel

Salesgirl: I need something to fill my hole. . . . [Quickly correcting herself when coworker stares.] I mean, something to fill the hole on the shelf. Someone bought all the baskets and now the shelf is empty.

*Crate & Barrel, Southdale Mall, Edina, Minnesota*

## When Donald Rumsfeld Goes Shopping

Suit: What is the difference between fiction and nonfiction?

*8820 American Way, Englewood, Colorado*

## Fortunately, We Have Robots to Do That Sort of Thing Now

Lab tech: So, Edwin* came up to me and was like, "What are you still doing here?" and I was like, "Oh my god, you gave me ten freakin' Western Blots to do. . . . What do you *think* I'm still doing here?" I mean, seriously—I was so tired I wanted to pipette myself to death.

*Merck and Company, West Point, Pennsylvania*


## EEOC: Ma'am, We Hear You Received a Comment on Your Box

Designer: You look Christmassy.
Writer: Christmassy?
Designer: Like a gift box. It's very nice.
Writer: A gift box. Huh. That's what I was going for.

*2001 Lind Avenue Southwest, Renton, Washington*


## You Said That Out Loud—Isn't That the First Clue That You're a Man?

Female VFX artist, about server: She's acting up again.
Male VFX artist #1: She? I always assumed it was male.
Male VFX artist #2: It's called Otis—isn't that the first clue that it's a man?
Male coworker: It's acting up—isn't that the first clue that it's a woman?

*San Francisco, California*

## Perv . . . -asive?

Gym junkie #1: Wow, you're good, you've been here every day this week.

Gym junkie #2: So have you, so I guess we're the same, then.

Gym junkie #1: Yeah, but I don't come here to work out every day.

Gym junkie #2: Oh, is there something else here?

Gym junkie #1: No, I'm just a perv.

*Movements Fitness Centre, Buranda Centro, Brisbane,*
*Australia*

## What Kind of Topping Do You Want?

Pizza guy: Hey, Jeff,* did you whisper my name?

Jeff: No.

Pizza guy: I must be hearing things. . . .

Jeff: I'll whisper your name if you want me to.

*Pizza place, Covington, Louisiana*

## Also My Definition of "Everywhere"

Man on cell and nearing exit: So you're where? I'm going to the exit. . . . [Two minutes later, in opposite direction] I've been looking everywhere for you! I looked in the women's restroom for you!

*Furniture store, Renton, Washington*

## Not Until Now, We Didn't

Safety officer to group of freshmen during orientation: Do you want to go to the fucking graveyard?! *No!*

*Crown College, University of California, Santa Cruz, California*

## . . . From the Backseat

Suit: Dude, you have to be careful when you drink and drive.

*475 Orange Street, Wilmington, North Carolina*

## At Least

Body piercer: Where do you work?
Piercee: At the *LA Weekly*.
Body piercer: Does that come out once a month?

*7274 Melrose Avenue, Los Angeles, California*

## They Earned It, Why Shouldn't They Hold It?

Chick hands clerk cash out of her bra.

Clerk: That's a safe place to keep money.
Chick: Them's the only two suckers I trust.

*Pawn shop, Fredericksburg, Virginia*

## And They Drive the Rest of Us to Suicide

City girl worker #1: Where were you this morning?
City girl worker #2: Oh, the trains were all up the wall again. Another fucking idiot jumped under a train during rush hour.
City girl worker #1: God, some people are so inconsiderate.

*Liverpool Street station, London, England*

## Come See the Softer Side of Nowhere

Little boy: We're in the middle of nowhere?
Mom: No, Danny.* We're in the middle of Sears.
Little boy: We're in the middle of nowhere!

*Sears, Huntington, New York*

## Yes, Despite Our Efforts to Eradicate It

Visiting professor: Is there a computer around here I can use to check my webmail?
Reception: You can use the one on the corner desk there.
Visiting professor: Will it have Google on it?

*South Melbourne, Australia*

## Go Easy on the Tongue, Though

Cook: What kind of fries would you like with that, ma'am?
Patron: French.

*Cottage Grove Road, Bloomfield, Connecticut*

## Didn't Realize I'd Be Working for Him

IT guy: I went to a Catholic school, so we were all extremely scared of Satan.

*Orlando, Florida*


## She's Got a Big Future in Health Care

Three-year-old daughter: Does it hurt?
Mom getting tattoo: Yeah, it hurts.
Three-year-old daughter: No, it doesn't.

*Ruby Street, Joliet, Illinois*


## Damn It! Me Am Artist!

Writer to designer: Sorry, the words have to make sense. I know, it sucks!

*2001 Lind Avenue Southwest, Renton, Washington*


## He Polishes Them Nightly

Warehouse guy: Hey, did you girls see my shiny nuts?

*8220 England Street, Charlotte, North Carolina*


## If It Isn't on *Punk'd*, It Doesn't Exist

Teacher introducing local news anchor: She's here to talk to you guys today about the media. And just recently, she won her first Emmy!
Student: What's that?

Local news anchor: [Bursts out laughing.]

*High school, Pflugerville, Texas*

## 'Cause This Is on Fire

Cautious electrician: I think they might have a first-aid kit up front.

Reckless electrician: I think I'm gonna go find out.

*333 North Meridian, Oklahoma City, Oklahoma*

## So You Know He Has Big Hands

Chubby female bar patron: Oh my god! That guy, like, totally just grabbed my ass.

*Center City, Philadelphia, Pennsylvania*

## Masculine Oranges

Band instructor: I need to ask you girls something, and I know who I am talking to. Okay . . . Do any of you girls have lotion—wait—that doesn't smell like girl?

Pit girl: Well, I have this sunscreen that smells like oranges. . . .

Band instructor: That just might work! Hit me with some.

*Intermediate school, Spring Grove, Pennsylvania*

## My Therapist Says I Have to Give Myself Permission to Make Mistakes

Chick #1: What'd you get?

Guy with lunch: Shrimp chowder.

Chick #1: Ew. Did that sound, like, appealing to you?

Guy with lunch: Yeah.

Chick #2: He likes shrimp.

Chick #1: I guess so. Hey, remember when you used to say "skrimp"?

Guy with lunch: Yeah.

Chick #1: You don't say "skrimp" anymore? That was just a phase?

Guy with lunch: Sometimes I still say "skrimp."

*Elevator, 1166 Avenue of the Americas, New York, New York*


## Bigfoot Is Pretty Cool, but I Don't Think Even He Can Control Evolution

Dude #1: See, you can't control evolution—it can't be controlled.

Dude #2: Oh, yeah? What about Bigfoot?

*College bookstore, North Carolina*


## No, She Just Pushed It

Girl peon #1: I haven't heard anything from Matt* all day. . . .

Girl peon #2: Get used to pushing that button a lot.

Girl peon #1: Been a long time for you, too, huh?

*4122 South Grove Road, Spokane, Washington*

## And So Osama bin Laden, Now a Bitter and Angry Man, Turned to a Life of Terrorism

Chief copy editor: Hey, what do you think of my turban? Think I can be a model in your hair supplement?

Beauty editor: What, the Bad Hair Day supplement?

*220 Loop Street, Cape Town, South Africa*

## Lawyer: That Would Have to Be *You*, Your Honor

Judge on conference call after everyone announced their appearance: Who represents God in this case? Everybody else has lawyers. . . .

*Roseville, California*

## How I Lost My Hand

Receptionist: You can't open a bag of Snickers in front of a fat woman!

*Elmhurst, Illinois*

## The Seductive Whir of the Cooling Fan Was Impossible to Resist

Techie holding computer: This thing is like, *so* fucked! Literally.

*New Orleans, Louisiana*

### . . . Dad

Worker on cell: And then my buttons got ripped, and I was like, "What are you doing? Yeah, it's cool in porno and all, but this is real life. . . ."

*Louisiana State University, Baton Rouge, Louisiana*

### Is Screaming All It Takes?

Woman looking over lunch menu: There's nothing here that's really screaming, "Eat me!" . . .

*Grand Avenue, El Segundo, California*

### I'm Allergic to Pol Pot and Idi Amin

Guy #1, looking out the window: Dude, weeds are boring.

Guy #2: What do you want me to do about it?

Guy #1: Well, you're the history major. Can't you ask them to name weeds after fascist dictators or something cool like that?

Guy #2: Yes . . . Yes, I can.

*Bellarmine University, Louisville, Kentucky*

### At the U.S. Treasury Department

Chick #1: I have such trouble with budgeting.

Chick #2: Yeah, me, too.

Chick #3: Actually, it's not the spending I have a problem with, it's paying it off.

*388 George Street, Sydney, Australia*

## Been Jobless Since He Wrote That Genius Snickers Commercial

Dude: Every time I don't eat I get hungry.

*Cafeteria, 1460 Broadway, New York, New York*

## Or Watching *Survivor*

Chick #1: Is there anything worse than having your period?
Chick #2: Having AIDS.

*Restroom, American University, Washington, DC*

## No, Stay Off! She's a Tease!

Man: She's blowing the thermostat and turning it on.

*High Street, Columbus, Ohio*

## Or We Could Agree to Blame the Romans

Jewish grad student: Wait, you're not Jewish! My people have been oppressed for thousands of years!
Catholic grad student: Yeah. And to be fair, my people did most of that oppressing.
Jewish grad student: Eh, we killed your god—let's call it even.

*Recruitment party, Princeton, New Jersey*

## Hey, If You Have People Who Dig That, Run with It!

Designer is eating a deli sandwich with a pickle sitting next to it.

Writer: I like your little pickle.
Designer, shaking his head: That's what they all tell me.

*260 Madison Avenue, New York, New York*

# ((contributors

Adam M, Amy, Andrew, Anne-Cara, Annmarie, Ashley, Astonished, Azn, bandgeek, Bartender Snickering Nearby, Becca, Becky, Beloislane, Beth, better the inbox than the outbox, Bill, Bored Beyond Belief, Brain Dancing, Brian Milvid, briarose, Brokeass Harem, Bruce R., burger lover, Catherine, CB, Charlotte, Chef, Cin, Citi Slicker, Collins, Cora, Cringing bartender, CSS Nightmare, CT Observer, Cube Farm Worker #5823457, Curious Kat, CytoToxicBlade, Dag, Dan, Dark_Kitty, David in Seattle, Dazed and confused, Debauched Angel, Deltar, Denise, Derek Paruolo, Donna, don't wanna go to it now, Dun Ben Ther, Elle, Emilio Lizardo, Emily, Emily Anne, english speaker, Evil twin, Ex-Employee, Extra Character, Fae, Fatty, Feeling Secure, Fellow Hallmark Employee, Fellow Teacher, Fellow worker sitting nearby, Firewall, FrancesDanger, Fransen comes alive, fred farqua, Fried Egg, Geobaldi, George Feeney, Gigi, Gilligan, Giselle, Gitcher Eyes Checked, Glinda Bright, Going to class, Grant, Grappling with zippers, Greggy, GregsBarandGrill, Guy at another table, Hang on voltaire, Harbor, Harriet Van, Herodotus420, Hiding in cubicle, Hitch, Hobo Whisperer, Home Depot Shopper, Hunger Pains, i like to eat too, Important cog, Innocent Bystander, Intern, IWNDRY, J. Max, Janie, JB, Jearu, Jen, Jenn, Jennifer Gerboth, Jess, JJK, Joe, Jonathan Willis, Jori, Julie, Juliloquy, Jullylully, June Bug, K-Mart Cashier, Kain, Kallisti, Karen, Kathryn, Kate, KilThor, Kim Siddorn, Krista, Lab rat, Lara, Lauren, Lauren Hopkins, Lee Hall, Lila, Lindsay, Luke, Manda b, Mark D., Marko, Marlous, Marshamellow, Mathwizrd, Matt, Mcbutters, McN, Meg, Meghan, Melessa, Melissa, Melvin, Meme, Miel, Mike, Mike Oxlong, Mikey Z, Milu, Mongo Man, Monika, Moron, Naomi, Needo, Never riding with the boss, Next in line, Non-profit ninja, Nosey, not a fan of November either, not a hole filler, Nurse says what, Office peon, Office peon/cubicle monkey, Outofstate, Over 30, Overworked, Painter, Pam Beasley, Peanut, Perpetrators, Petyr, Playtah, Poj, Poor Guy, Pop Culturally Literate, Potitia, Praying for Death, Prefekt, Probably going to hell also, Pu-King, Quitting soon, R. Smith, R U Shittin' Me, Random Eavesdropper, Ranga Tobious, Raydran, Recovering Workaholic, Redstick Zero Five, Reed, Ren, Renjeau, Rhymes with Banana, Rich, Ryan, Sam, Samantha Edith Hansen, Sandie, Sara, Sarah, Sarah Cullen, Sassafrass, SB, Scott, SeeNoSpeakNo, Shaking Head, Shannon, Shatmandu, She's Not Psychic, Shenanigan, Shrek, Smithout, Smooth, Snark Monster, Snoopdude, Snoopervisor, Spacing Out, Speechless, Speechless RN, Steak of life, Stefanie, Stephanie, Stephen, Still Giggling, Still laughing now, Stretch, Surrounded by stupid, Suse, Tara, Tits McGee, The Best and the Brightest, The fly on the wall, The Intern, The Lurker, The Man, The new trout, The Office Boy, The

Temp, The Yeti, Thompson, Trey Givens, Tricky Nikki, Trish, Twelve step, Underpaid TA, Vagina warrior, Very Disturbed, Vicky, Vinyl Junkie, Volks, Walking Along, Web monkey, Why Me?, Whyamlhere?, Will, will1966, WOW@CU, Writer and consumer, Wscnsngl, Xanadon't it, Xen, Yank Down Under, You've got to be kidding me!, and Zarbettu

# ((about the authors

**S. Morgan Friedman** originated various popular websites, including Walking Around, WordCounter, the Cliché Finder, the Inflation Calculator, and Cyranet. Morgan founded Diseño Porteño, a graphic design and software development firm. He is also a graduate of the University of Pennsylvania.

**Michael Malice** is the subject of Harvey Pekar's *Ego & Hubris: The Michael Malice Story*. He is also the coauthor of the forthcoming autobiography of UFC champion Matt Hughes, titled *Made in America*.